WHY YOU SHOULD INVEST YOUR MONEY AND TIME IN THIS BOOK!

Mr. Chenthil R. Iyer has written an essential book on personal finance which answers many questions you didn't know whom to ask and also questions you should have asked but didn't know you needed the answers to!
The book is an easy read, devoid of jargon, using interesting examples. Chenthil has made a dry subject interesting, often lacing his comments with subtle humour.
He has covered a vast canvas covering topics ranging from the habit of saving to investing, providing for current needs to planning for retirement, the pros and cons of buying real estate and investing in equity and many others.
The good part is that he dishes out his advice in bite-sized portions, that are not only easy to eat but also to digest.
I liked a statement Chenthil has used at the end of one of the chapters, 'If you can work 5-6 days a week to generate money, you better spend a few hours a month to manage it!'
All in all, a must read, particularly for those about to begin their career, people with fixed incomes struggling to balance the myriad demands on their money, and anyone wishing to fine-tune the nuances of money management.

- Dr Anil Lamba, Director – Lamcon &
Author of *Romancing the Balance Sheet*

Money - what a lovely world we get into, when we hear this word. Chenthil has given a good way to think about money and personal finances through the journey of Subbu in the book, 'Everyone has an eye on your wallet, do you?'
I have read many books on personal finances, but this book cuts across all other books, because it is simple for a beginner and offers profound insights for the experienced ones. I recommend to not just read, but re-read and recommend this book to others as well.
Sure to see this book on the best seller list.

Dr. Radhakrishnan Pillai,
Author of *Corporate Chanakya*

Chenthil's book is a must read for anyone who wishes to take charge of his or her finances. Chenthil is himself an acclaimed financial advisor but there's a phrase in Hindi which goes "khudke marey bagair swarg nahin milta," - one can't attain heaven without giving up ones own life first. In that context I don't see how anyone can become financially strong without taking charge personally and getting into the nuances of money management - maybe that's why a financial advisor has given you this opportunity; sharing all his insights selflessly for you to learn from. He has laid down the entire subject of personal finance by way of simple stories, practical examples, anecdotes and a dash of philosophy where relevant! At the same time demonstrating practical calculations with "how to" formulae goes a long way to empower the reader. A plan discussed with your advisor doesn't look the same in flesh and blood (read numbers and arithmetic). Hence I recommend you to read the entire book and try out some of the number crunching for yourself. It promises to be an eye opener; don't worry when it does! There's another saying "jahaan jaage wahin savera", the moment you wake up, that's morning for you! So get going.

- Aashish Somaiya,
CEO of Motilal Oswal AMC

In this age of information overload, high-pitched promotions and bombarding salesmen, Chenthil Iyer's book equips investors with an easy to understand and simple to implement strategy which can help them to achieve financial freedom and a sense of peace around money!
What makes the book more meaningful & practical is the author's financial planning practice background of helping hundreds of investors achieve their financial goals in life through one-to-one coaching, seminars & workshops.
The chapters are neatly categorized covering the entire gamut of personal finance and the concepts are explained in an interesting way using practical cases and stories around the character, Subbu. This is a must read book for every investor who does not want to be taken for a ride by financial service companies.

- Sadique Neelgund CFP^{CM},
Founder & CEO - Network FP

An important addition to the personal finance and financial literacy space in India.

-Monika Halan
Consulting Editor, Mint - HT Media

EVERYONE HAS AN EYE ON **YOUR WALLET!** DO YOU?

CHENTHIL R. IYER

This edition first published in 2017

Published in India by:
Embassy Book Distributors
120, Great Western Building,
Maharashtra Chamber of Commerce Lane,
Fort, Mumbai - 400 023.
Tel : (91-22) 22819546 / 22818567.
Email : info@embassybooks.in
Website : www.embassybooks.in

Distribution Centres:
Mumbai, Bangalore, Kolkata, Chennai,
Hyderabad, New Delhi, Pune

ISBN: 978-93-86450-50-0

Typesetting and Layout by PSV Kumarasamy

DEDICATIONS

Dedicated to my mother, who instilled very high standards of values in me of honesty and integrity; who proved to me that a family of four can be run effectively on a meagre income and taught me the virtue of frugality; who took financial risks as per the need of the hour while saving lovingly and meticulously for her children's future at the very high cost of her personal comforts.

Dedicated to my sisters who always believed in me and provided me with the much needed support and encouragement in every way throughout my entrepreneurial journey, which I still consider to have just begun; who trusted me repeatedly after every failure, even when my mother had given up on me!

Dedicated to my wife, who was the first one to tell me 'You should write a book'; who always dreamt of a showcase full of books authored by me, when I used to write just two-pager articles; whom I would wake up in the middle of the night when I'd get a 'wonderful' idea; who wouldn't get bored even when I would excitedly ask her to read the umpteenth correction of a paragraph and give me her honest feedback.

Dedicated to all my client-friends who believed in me when I proposed to give them truly 'unbiased' financial advice and always treated me like a family member.

ACKNOWLEDGEMENTS

The idea of writing a book is so very different from actually writing a book. You always need that extra push. That is what I got when I attended an Author Workshop by Mr. Nitin Soni of Adhyyan Publications. I thank him for that inspirational workshop in which he explained how a non-fiction book can be written in as short a period as 21 days! And on the very same night, I jotted down the points that have got converted into the various chapters of this book.

The next step was to find a publisher, as being a first time author I wasn't too confident about self-publishing. That was when I spoke to my dear friend Manish Kulkarni who organizes regular events around books as part of a CSR activity of the company he works for. I thank him for connecting me to Sohin Lakhani of Embassy Books. Sohin is such a sweet person to talk to and is a great friend to have. We connected almost instantly and within a couple of weeks their editor Aruna Joshi reverted with the proposal to publish. I thank the entire Embassy Books team for being such great people to work with!

Creating the character Subbu was an interesting experience. I have been using this 'formless' character for over 2 years in my workshop for children called 'Money Is Child's Play.' The Subbu stories I narrated in these workshops made learning about money a fun experience for those children, a topic often avoided even by adults! Many parents also loved those stories and suggested that the stories should be shared with the masses. I thank those children and parents for participating in this humble endeavour of creating a financially aware future generation.

Now it was time to give a form to Subbu! How do you get such a character made at an optimum cost without compromising the quality? That is when a friend of mine suggested Fiverr and I decided to try it. I found the work of Christobal Mikhov, who operates there in the name of Cartoonwizzard impressive and engaged him for the task. And this amazingly talented artist understood my description of Subbu so well and gave him the much needed form. I thank Christobal Mikhov for such a wonderful effort.

Since Fiverr made my life easy, it became my first choice to create a few other graphics as well. I thank Joe Chyna who operates in the name of chyna_creatives for helping me with the front cover design as well as a couple of graphics. I thank Sauvagya Bhanja, who operates in the name srbhanja for helping me with some of the graphics.

Special thanks to all the lovely people who welcomed me wholeheartedly and readily agreed to take out the time to review the manuscript and offered their valuable comments and words of encouragement.

Thank you Dr. Anil Lamba, Dr. Radhakrishnan Pillai, Mr. Aashish Somaiya, Mr. Sadique Neelgund and my dear client-friend, Mr. Hemant Deshpande!

Most importantly, I thank my wife Supriya for inspiring me to become an author. She has read each line that I have written for the book and every revision that I have made without losing an ounce of interest. Since I was writing a personal finance book for laymen, I needed a guinea pig to test whether what I wrote could be understood by them! She willingly became that for me and after reading every paragraph, she would just smile at me and say if she understood it or not; simple.

I don't know if I can fill a showcase with my books, but I surely know that I have made a beginning; So I thank myself for that!

The acknowledgements would be incomplete without thanking the Almighty Lord Krishna for coming into my life in the form of all these wonderful people mentioned above and making this work a reality.

CONTENTS

PREFACE

"Blessed are you who are poor, for you do not have to worry about spending or investing money."

– *Anonymous*

From the time you get out of bed, till you get back to it, you encounter all sorts of sales pitches from those who are eyeing a share of your wallet. While some are suggesting you can live a better life by using their products or services, others are telling you where to invest. There is yet another set of people luring you with 'awesome' bargains and there are many others who are offering you something of value absolutely FREE!

Whether you tune into any television or radio channel, or open the newspaper or even social media platforms, you will find direct or indirect references that influence your buying or investment decisions. Not to mention the direct approaches that sellers make through unsolicited telephone calls and emails.

How do you cut through all this clutter and get to what you exactly want to use your money for? This requires you to have a clear understanding of the various financial concepts, at least at the level of being able to take rational decisions.

Unfortunately, in the nearly 20 years of schooling that an average urban individual goes through, nothing is taught to him about personal finance. After that, life takes over and imparts those money lessons in a hard way, and that too, over a prolonged period of time.

Ever heard 'You have to be duped by someone to get wiser?' Really? Maybe but maybe not if you invest the time and make some efforts to understand the nuances of personal finance.

I still clearly remember how I got duped by a stranger when I had just joined my first job. After a few initial encounters, he asked me for a loan of 2,000 rupees and gave me a post-dated (dated a month later) cheque for the same amount in return. I obliged him immediately as I felt that there was no risk involved since I had his cheque in hand. A warning bell rang in my head when I noticed that he had not signed the cheque. When I brought it to his notice, he told me that it was a special account and did not require a signature. And I, a distinction holder in B.Tech, Mechanical Engineering, believed him! I still have that cheque with me, a copy of which is reproduced below.

This event literally blew my head off and proved to me beyond doubt that your academic intelligence has nothing to do with the awareness of your personal finance!

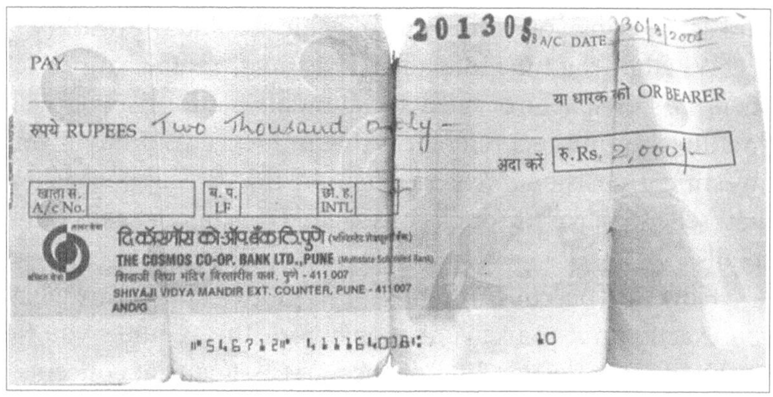

201305 A/C DATE 30/3/2001

PAY

या धारक को OR BEARER

रुपये RUPEES Two Thousand only -

अदा करें रु.Rs. 2,000/-

खाता सं. A/c No. | ब. प. LF | छो. ह. INTL

THE COSMOS CO-OP. BANK LTD., PUNE

SHIVAJI VIDYA MANDIR EXT. COUNTER, PUNE - 411007

AND/G

⑈546712⑈ 411164008⑆ 10

I would like to thank this gentleman, wherever he is, for that experience marked the beginning of my journey into the field of personal finance which eventually became my career.

Today, not only are my own finances in good shape, but I have also been able to help many people gain control over theirs. Read on, and I am sure you will be able to take control of yours too!

Introducing Subbu...

Subbu is a simpleton in his mid-20s without much practical knowledge. He tends to commit errors that defy common sense. Throughout this book we will keep looking into his life. Some events from Subbu's life may seem to be idiotic, but in an entertaining way, they teach us some fundamental aspects related to the way we deal with money and our behaviour towards it. These lessons from Subbu may subconsciously guide us in the right direction at the time of taking various practical financial decisions.

1

SPENDING – A PLEASURABLE EXPERIENCE

"All income and little expense made Subbu a dull man."
– *A modified English proverb*

Subbu lived carelessly for most of his life. But his father's untimely demise made him excessively cautious about money. There came a phase in his life when he would save almost every penny he earned, which he kept safe in a locker in his bedroom, barely spending on his necessities. He developed an obsession for money and religiously counted all his money before sleeping every night. Somehow it made him feel secure and happy. One night as he opened the safe, he found to his horror that all the money had disappeared! A thief had robbed him of all his life savings. And in the place of his bundles of cash, were kept bundles of newspaper neatly cut in the shape of currency notes. Also, there was a note stuck inside the safe which read, "If it is only counting you have to do every night, these newspaper bundles should work just as well!"

Most financial planners dissuade their clients from spending money. As a result most people end up feeling guilty about spending. However, if you go a little deeper, you will understand that you get paid *only* when someone else spends his or her money. So folks, don't fret over spending money. I am not a great shopper myself and I like being frugal. However, when I *really* want something, I go ahead and buy it and feel good about doing so.

Let me ask you a question. How many of you enjoy brushing your teeth every morning? Did I hear a naaaah.. or you don't even remember brushing your teeth, since it is a habit you barely pay attention to, right?

You may be thinking, 'Hey, what does this have to do with spending?' The pleasure in any activity is sustained only when it does not become routine. If you become habituated to spending money on anything other than essentials, even shopping would no longer remain a pleasure. However routine it may seem, you will still do it, with the hope that your next purchase will make you happy. And that's where things get out of control.

Each time you buy something, it should make you feel happier than before. That feel-good hormone should rush through your blood, leaving you with a feeling of exhilaration. And more importantly, you are also contributing to creating a healthy and vibrant economy. However, it is very important to learn how to make a good buying decision. The two main parameters that decide the quality of a buying decision are 'value' and 'cost.' Value represents the degree of utility that you derive from a product or service, whereas the cost represents the amount of money you end up paying for getting a specific value. This combination between value and cost may be represented in the form of a quadrant which I would like to call as the Buyer's Utility Windows. Value is plotted on the x-axis and cost on the y-axis. This creates four windows of varying cost and value.

BUYER'S UTILITY WINDOWS

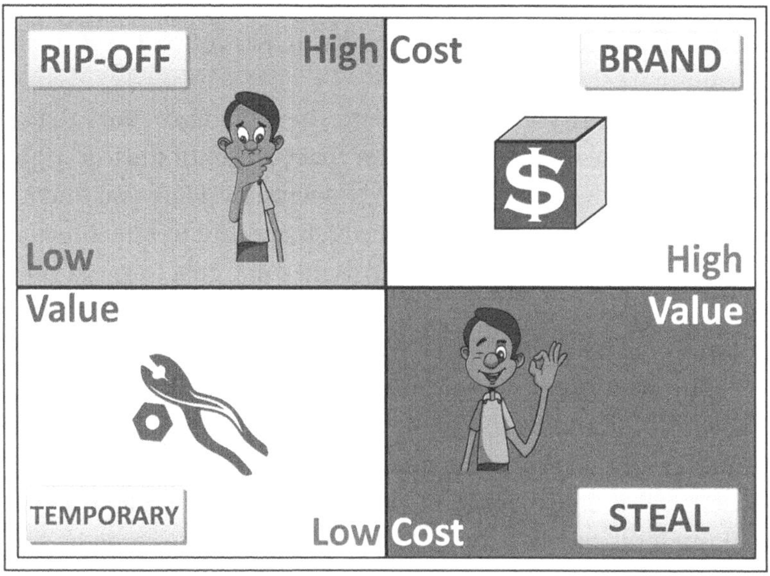

RIP-OFF
High Cost
BRAND
Low
High
Value
Value
TEMPORARY
Low Cost
STEAL

The most important window is the bottom right one, as it represents low cost and high value. The utility to the buyer is the maximum in this window. That's why I have named this window as the STEAL window. Any purchase that falls in this category gives you the maximum pleasure and happiness. However, making such value purchases requires you to spend sufficient time and effort in terms of comparing and contrasting various options, not only from the price point of view but also from a technical perspective. For example, instead of buying a standard packaged music system that may look great, it could be really cheap if you know how to assemble one by buying the various components. This may not 'look' great but would definitely 'sound' great as it is highly unlikely that all the components manufactured by the same company are the best. Add to this the additional pleasure of showing off your self-created possession. Alternatively, there is a possibility that a relatively unknown company manufactures a better product in a particular category and is offering it at a lower cost as it wants to gain market share.

However, if you cannot spend the time and effort that a value purchase requires, it is better that you go for the top -right window, which is called the BRAND window. Here you find all established high-quality brands which are safe to buy albeit at a higher cost. However, if you attribute some cost towards your time and effort, which the BRAND window saves, utility-wise it may come near the STEAL window.

The window to avoid is the top-left one. This is named the RIP-OFF and as the name suggests, consists of low-value products and services that are offered at very high costs. There exists such a 'con-market' in every industry which focuses on making fools out of people. Many such products come to you through alternative marketing routes such as doorstep selling, social media, fly by night Multi-Level-Marketing companies, late night television infomercials or e-commerce market places, where it becomes quite confusing and difficult to benchmark, the quality or pricing. Not all products sold through these channels are a rip-off, but it would pay to exercise caution in such markets, especially if they are offering quick-fix solutions for otherwise complex problems.

The bottom-left window is the low-value – low-cost one, which is aptly titled as TEMPORARY, indicating those products or services that you may need just on a transitory note. The products that you may need for a festival period of just a week or so after which they may lose their utility or be discarded, could be a great example for this window.

Hence it is very important that you apply the Buyer's Utility Window test before making a buying decision and select the appropriate strategy in a given situation. In addition, given below are some pointers that will help you to keep your expenditure on track.

Impulsive Buying – If you go to a market place, physical or virtual, and the moment you see an ad flashing, or you see the product attractively presented in the display window, you are tempted to buy it, there is a reason to worry; because you are acting on your impulse. In such a case you can practice what is called as 'Delayed Gratification.' You may check out the product, but don't buy until a few days pass by. If you postpone your buying decision consciously by a week or two, your mind will get the time to process the idea and figure out whether it will really add value to you or not.

Track Your Expenses – The awareness of how much is being spent is the best way to apply brakes on your spending, unless you have suicidal tendencies! Here I am not talking about jotting down every rupee that you spend. There can be two major categories, cash expenses and digital expenses, thanks to the demonetization initiative. Wherever you can use your digital wallets, cards or various payment apps (keep one in each category to avoid complication), do not use cash. This way, you can reduce your cash expenses to a minimum and bulk of the expenses gets automatically tracked digitally. Also you can track your cash expenses through the ATM withdrawals that you make.

Credit cards however can be a tricky affair sometimes. They can create a tendency to spend more when you can actually do with less. It is strange but true that people are able to restrain themselves when they have to give out currency notes or use debit cards, but become extravagant and generous when they spend through a credit card. Possibly because they have to pay that off using future income, with which they haven't established an emotional connect yet! However, the money in one's account seems more valuable. Therefore you have to be extremely cautious when using your credit cards and could choose to keep the credit limit just sufficient enough to accommodate two to three months of budgeted expenses.

A word of caution to those who have cash income and therefore would like to spend in cash:

If your income is unaccounted, your expenses also would be unaccounted. And that would eventually lead to a much bigger loss than the taxes you save. We will discuss this in detail in a chapter dedicated to this topic.

Save tax on your expenditure; Don't create unnecessary expenditure to save tax!

Ever heard the phrase, 'putting the cart before the horse' or 'the tail wagging the dog?'

That is exactly what I say about all the people I have met in my career who are on a tax-saving spree. Most of the tax-saving avenues require you to spend money first or lock up your money for a very long term. For example, you get a tax break on interest paid on a housing loan. This interest is actually an expense. However, purchasing a house is a financial goal that needs to be feasible, considering your current and prospective financial situations. Those people who jump into taking a home loan just for the sake of saving tax, mostly end up having a very tough financial situation and eventually spend money using very expensive means such as credit cards and personal loans with interest rates upwards of 15-18%. That is being penny wise and pound foolish, isn't it?

To all these people my advice would be to stay in a rented house of their choice until their financials grow strong and they can comfortably afford to buy a house without disturbing their financial situation. In the Indian context, rentals are much cheaper than the interest on home loan, and both are expenditures. And you do get a tax break on the House Rent Allowance component of your salary.

For those who think that paying EMIs is equivalent to investing, my humble submission is that the interest component of the EMI is an expense and since the loan amount is high in the initial half of the repayment tenure, the principal repayment forms a minuscule investment.

However, if a rational expenditure or investment you make, attracts a tax benefit, by all means grab it. Tax benefits should be just a by-product of financially prudent decisions instead of being the primary objective.

Ask yourself, 'Do I really deserve it?'

Many a times, our emotions play spoilsport in our endeavour towards fiscal prudence. After a hard week's toil at work, it is but natural to feel like pampering yourself. You may want to visit a mall, splurge on stuff for yourself and your home, dine at a restaurant, or watch a movie. But your pampering and your actual need may not be in sync. What you really need is adequate rest and relaxation at the sweetest place on earth, your home. But how to ward off all those weekend getaway advertisements you see on the internet? All those nice restaurants with great ambience that would run dry if not for you; and all those movies that get released on weekends hoping that you would be there on time!

If you think I am against all of these pleasurable things in life, please go back to the beginning of this chapter. I am sure that all those who overdo the above stuff on weekends have one thing in common. They all very much believe they deserve it. But I believe they deserve better! They are all victims of social conditioning, the most predominant one being the 'work hard party harder' philosophy. Every professional athlete knows the importance of rest and recuperation. So is the case for a knowledge worker.

If you hit the work desk on Monday morning tired and frustrated, you have only yourself to blame.

At a glance . . .

- ₹ *Any spending that you do should make you feel happier than before.*
- ₹ *Every time you make an expense, you are contributing to creating a healthy and vibrant economy.*
- ₹ *Value represents the degree of utility that you derive from a product or service.*
- ₹ *Cost represents the amount of money you end up paying for getting a specific value.*
- ₹ *Apply the Buyer's Utility Window test before making a buying decision.*
- ₹ *Practice 'Delayed Gratification.'*
- ₹ *Using digital mode wherever possible for expenditure helps you track it more effectively and efficiently.*
- ₹ *If your income is unaccounted, your expenses also would be unaccounted.*
- ₹ *Tax benefits should be a by-product of financially prudent decisions and not the primary objective.*
- ₹ *How your heart will ask you to pamper yourself is so very different from what you actually need.*

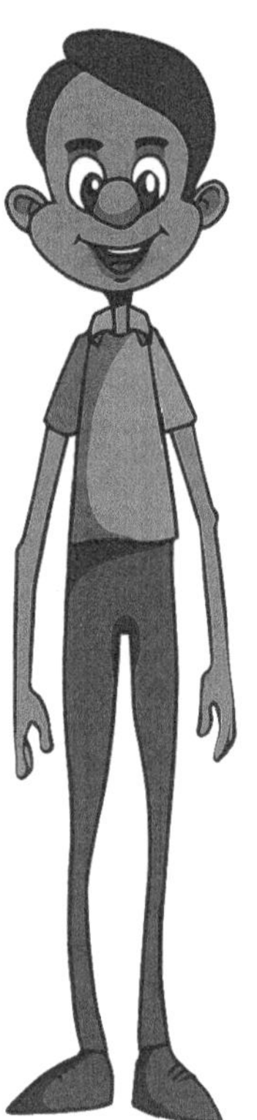

2

ADVERTISING – THE ART OF CREATING NEED

"History will see advertising as one of the real evil things of our time. It is stimulating people constantly to want things, want this, want that."

– Malcolm Muggeridge

Subbu won a lottery for Rs.1,000 and after collecting his prize money he went to watch a movie. Before the start of the movie an advertisement flashed showing golden corn being made into fluffy salted popcorn and everyone enjoying the movie with a tub of popcorn in their hands. He had never eaten popcorn ever in his life and when he looked around, a lot of people were having it. And soon another advertisement flashed about a movie ticket booking app which was offering a discount of 50% on popcorn upon booking the tickets through them. 'Maybe you have to eat popcorn while watching movies!' he thought, but resisted. He knew he had already spent a lot of his prize money. The movie began and he forgot about the popcorn. During the interval, the first slide that came up had the caption, "Haven't you picked up your popcorn yet?" with the picture of a tub overflowing with yummy looking popcorn. It was as if there was someone watching him and talking to him directly! That was it. He went out, spent whatever money he had and got his tub of popcorn.

Advertising has long evolved from being a mere announcement that a product exists, to engaging people into a psychological narrative that leads them into seriously feeling the lack of it, garnished with a dash of entertainment. However, the entertainment works only in the initial few encounters after which it becomes plain boring. The real game begins at this point. The catch phrases, jingles, freebies, limited period offers etc. start playing in your mind even without your conscious awareness. The higher the number of repetitions of the advertisement you are exposed to, the higher the recall value of the product.

An average individual spends around two hours in front of the television, thirty minutes reading the newspaper, close to an hour commuting and listening to FM radio, and another hour on social networking sites and the internet. That's a phenomenal amount of time to get bombarded with advertisements of all shapes and sizes. We always think we have made a choice to buy, but the truth is that we have almost always been influenced, if not coerced into making those choices. The advertisers are the Pied Pipers of the modern era and we are all deeply enchanted by their music. If you find yourself being 'brand-conscious' instead of being 'value-conscious' as explained in the previous chapter, be rest assured that you have been caught in the web of smart advertisers. The more advertising one does, the bigger the brand value and its recall.

We should take conscious and special efforts to reduce the impact these advertisements make on us. They tend to create more needs than required and leave us with a feeling of severe deficiency that can not only seriously jeopardize our finances but also our emotions; and in some extreme cases may even lead to psychological disorders including depression. The best approach would be to look for options and take well- thought-out decisions when needs naturally arise, instead of becoming a victim of the ad-mad world! There are some genuinely creative people in the ad industry, who come up with entertaining commercials once in a while. Do enjoy them as and when they come, but ensure that you do not fall prey to them.

Here are a few important steps you can take to minimize the influence of advertisements and protect your wallet from unnecessary expenditures.

While watching TV, keep the remote in your hand and hit the mute button the moment commercials start flashing. You need to consciously train yourself in doing this so that you don't miss your programs and also don't get overwhelmed by the ads. You will never be efficient with this trick and therefore will not miss out on the entertainment aspect of the ads either and will be just 'informed' about the various products whenever you slip on this challenge. Alternatively you may watch recorded programs of your interest and fast-forward the advertisements.

Most of us barely read enough these days (The book you are holding in your hand was too good for you to miss and therefore an exception!). So keep a book near you while watching television. The moment you hit the mute button, pick up the book and start reading. With some trial and error, you can find the average number of pages you will finish by the time the ad break gets over and look up only upon finishing those many pages. You may miss a few scenes until you get this right, but the rewards are multifold. In fact you get, on an average, 15-20 such free minutes in every hour of television program. Imagine how many books you would read in a year while watching television!

Keep a memory stick full of songs. Its okay to buy songs, as a lot of effort goes into creating them. If they are giving you the entertainment you need while commuting to work and back, they deserve to get paid a one-time fee. You can intermittently fill it with audio-books, motivational and educational seminars etc. and listen on a shuffle mode so that along with entertainment you will be adding more value to yourself and the suspense of what comes next is also kept intact. Keep updating the list of songs and other audio files on a weekly or monthly basis so that the variety and interest are kept alive. And one more thing is guaranteed - you will smile your way through the traffic and reduce your stress levels substantially.

But if you are in love with the husky, sexy voice of your favourite RJs, then flip the channel as soon as the ad break comes. The FM radio channels have become so smart that almost all channels have ad breaks at the same time, especially during the peak hours. *Vividh Bharti* is quite a safe option to switch to in such moments of crisis, and if that also doesn't help, hit the mute button!

Newspapers and social media have very limited influence on us as they do not hold us back from flipping through the pages or closing the pop-ups; unlike television and radio where the programs continue only after the compulsory ad break. You tend to look further into the ad only if the first 2-3 seconds are of interest to you. You may use an effective pop-up blocker to avoid getting the pop-up advertisements on the social media and the internet. You may also subscribe to those newspapers which have minimal ads.

Exercise these real choices that you have and you are well on your way towards financial well-being. The motto is to protect your brain and wallet at any cost - ironical though!

The trouble however, is to control oneself when our close friend or neighbour flaunts her new acquisition. That is nothing but what we call in behavioural terms as *peer pressure.* Some stranger becoming a big shot, or doing something out of the world may be no big deal for most of us. But someone known to you does it, and if your heart feels a sense of envy and a part of you wants to emulate it, you are a victim of peer pressure. Social media has only added fuel to this fire. Every day you see someone or the other travelling abroad, buying a new car, watching a movie or a live game, and you are thinking 'what am I doing here?'

Handling peer pressure starts with the realization that everyone is living their own unique lives and goes through their fair share of ups and downs. While it is okay to be 'inspired' by other people's accomplishments, it will be very wrong to try and emulate others in every way one can with an unhealthy and negative spirit of competition and one-upmanship. It will be a good idea to actually count your blessings every day and be grateful for what you already have, since it's a very good possibility that a lot of people in your circle are actually aspiring for the very same things that you may be taking for granted!

At a glance . . .

- ₹ *We always think we have made a choice to buy, but the truth is that we have almost always been influenced, if not coerced into making those choices.*
- ₹ *Look for options and take a calculated decision when a need naturally arises, instead of becoming a victim of the ad-mad world.*
- ₹ *While watching TV, keep the remote in your hand and hit the mute button the moment ads start flashing.*
- ₹ *Keep a book near you while watching television and as the ad break starts, pick up the book and start reading.*
- ₹ *Keep a memory stick full of songs and use it more often than the FM radio.*
- ₹ *Use an effective pop-up blocker while surfing the internet and subscribe to newspapers having minimal ad content.*
- ₹ *Be conscious of peer pressure. Think before you want to blindly emulate someone.*

3

BEING PENNY WISE & POUND FOOLISH; WHAT FORMAL EDUCATION HAS NOTHING TO DO WITH

"Wisdom comes from within. Knowledge is acquired and can sometimes put a screen on your wisdom."

– A. R. Rahman

It was getting dark. Subbu remembered about the power shutdown scheduled for the evening and rushed to the shop to buy a candle and a match box. 'The candle is for three rupees and the match box is for one rupee,' said the shopkeeper. Subbu handed out a five rupee coin and got the change of one rupee which he put into his pocket. On the way back he heard a clinking sound and checked his pocket. The one rupee coin had slipped out through a hole in his pocket. He felt bad losing the one rupee and it was too dark for him to search. Then an idea struck him. He took out the match box, lit the candle and started looking for the coin, priding himself for his intelligence. After a search of about half an hour he found it. But to his dismay, he found that he had burnt the candle out in the process!

Such situations arise quite regularly in our lives where we think we are saving money but in fact we are spending or losing much more money. Many a time, it is not a 'money for money' story, but money for health, money for time etc. If you don't believe this, take a trip to the local vegetable market and observe people buying veggies and fruits. You may see people haggle for 5 rupees and 10 rupees as if their life depends on it. The same evening they may visit an expensive restaurant and pay 500 rupees or 1000 rupees for a portion of vegetable! How much ever they may defend this expense to be for the ambience and not for the vegetables, we all know deep down in our hearts that it is too much to pay compared to the savings they made in the morning. I have even heard arguments that the restaurant expense is a once-in-a-while affair whereas bargaining for vegetables is a daily routine. However, such 'once in a while' spending runs many times over the small savings we claim to make. The issue is not whether to bargain at the market or not. Neither is the issue about spending large amounts at a restaurant. It is about the halo that we carry about ourselves of being financially prudent when we save a few pennies here and there while spending huge amounts without much thought. Add to that the feeling of saving some money making us 'eligible' to splurge once in a while, and the self-deception becomes complete!

There are other examples such as the long queues we see outside petrol pumps when the fuel price is expected to increase by a rupee from midnight. People spend close to an hour standing in the queue and all they can fill is 15-20 litres, saving them a total of 20 rupees! Probably they would have burnt that much petrol switching their cars on and off while waiting for their turn. Or that one hour could have been time well-spent with the family that got compromised for a mere 20 rupees!

Fast-food joints have combo meals that give you a feel of a value deal, but quite possibly you just need one of the items that would have been cheaper if purchased separately. However, in your eagerness to save money, you end up consuming that unwanted drink or those extra fries! Shopping malls also offer you such deals combining a fast-moving item with two other slow-moving items which you may not need at present. But from their MRP they will be available at attractive discounts. And you convince yourself that since you may need those in the future, why not buy them cheap and keep. Every household has a lot of such things dumped in the lofts that are still waiting to be used in future! Most of those don't see the light of day and end up being sold as junk.

Those of you who are big fans of 'used' products such as vehicles or electronic gadgets may very well be prepared for escalating cost of future repairs and maintenance unless you are technically proficient in terms of finding that real value deal after conducting sufficient due diligence.

The most critical behaviour of this kind happens when it comes to pure insurance plans. A term insurance plan may cost just a few thousand rupees a year for a substantial amount of cover. However, people look to save this money and buy insurance for a lesser amount in endowment-type policies that promise some guaranteed returns. In the event of the person's death, the family ends up getting an amount that is grossly insufficient to take care of their financial goals. The main argument against term plans is that nothing comes back. However the fact is that every insurance policy has mortality charges bundled into its cost structure, which may not be transparently revealed in all cases. This is dealt with in detail in a later chapter.

Whether it is the decision about doing a part-time course to enhance your skills or one related to consuming organic foods that may cost more than the other alternatives, they all have long-ranging impact either in terms of earning you substantial additional income or protecting you from major health hazards due to pesticides and insecticides respectively. The act of saving money in such instances will only result in huge losses resulting from missed opportunities that may otherwise open up due to your possession of additional skills, or in terms of huge hospital bills towards treatment of degenerative diseases that may even reduce the quality of life post-treatment!

From a global perspective, the burning of fossil fuels instead of using renewable resources such as solar energy thinking that fossil fuels are cheaper is by far the most foolish decision ever made by the human race. The environmental impact of such a decision can be so devastating that it has the potential to wipe out the entire life on Earth. Similar is the case when we use plastic as a cheaper alternative to other biodegradable, but 'expensive' materials.

On a lighter side, there may be many who will not buy this book and save some money and try to gain all this information online in an unstructured manner and eventually fall prey to sales pitches and end up losing a lot of money. (That may sound like a sales pitch too; but you are the judge.) 'Thoughtful spending' and 'informed saving', understanding clearly the consequences of both, are two integral habits one needs to cultivate in order to avoid being penny wise and pound foolish.

At a glance . . .

- ₹ *Penny wise and pound foolish behaviour need not always be a 'money for money' story. It can be money for health, money for time etc. as well.*
- ₹ *Saving some money here and there doesn't necessarily make us 'eligible' to splurge once in a while.*
- ₹ *Combo deals don't necessarily save you money; many a time they make your home a junkyard.*
- ₹ *Second-hand products or used goods may be cheap but may turn out to be expensive if you do not have the necessary know-how.*
- ₹ *Spend money on pure insurance of all kinds. If that money is lost, it's a good loss to make.*
- ₹ *Never save money at the cost of a large opportunity.*
- ₹ *Cultivate the habits of 'thoughtful spending' and 'informed saving.'*

4

MAKING THE DRAMATIC SHIFT FROM 'I – E = S' TO 'I – S = E'

"All expense and little income made Subbu a broke man."

– English proverb further modified

Remember Subbu had won a lottery? Here's the full story. The prize money was of 1,000 rupees. *In order to claim the money he had to go to their office the next day and show his ticket. He couldn't sleep that night as he was obsessed with his new-found wealth. He thought to himself, 'I will put this money in the bank and it will earn interest and then the interest will earn interest and after some time I will have 2,000* rupees *in my account.' Next morning, as he stepped out of his home, he felt like a king. He was rich, and didn't know how to show it to his neighbours. The lottery office was just a few kilometres away and on any other day he would have walked that distance, but today was different. 'A little luxury won't do much harm. It's not every day that people win lotteries,' he told himself and called for a taxi. Soon he was on his way to the lottery office enjoying a taxi ride. He stopped the car in front of his friend Ramu's house. Ramu was standing outside watering his plants. Subbu called out to him, 'Ramu, I won a lottery and am going to collect the money. Would you like to join me?' And the two friends happily were on their way. Upon reaching the office, Subbu showed the ticket to the officer who verified it and handed over the cash, congratulating him on his win. When he counted the money, it was only 700* rupees *and so he asked the officer for the remaining money. The officer replied, 'We have deducted the tax as per rules. Can't help it!' Subbu was sad, but soon perked himself up. He still had a lot of money after all. Ramu was waiting in the car and upon seeing Subbu come out, got out of the car and told him, 'Congratulations! Let's celebrate this.' And they went to a nice restaurant and had their heart's fill. The bill amount? 200* rupees. *The waiter was so nice and showed tremendous hospitality. 'Got to give a tip!' thought Subbu and put another 20 rupees on the table.*

As they were on their way back home, Subbu saw the poster of a newly released movie flashing by and felt like watching it. Ramu was also game, and off they went to the cinema. Subbu let the taxi go as the movie would take a couple of hours. So off went another 150 rupees. After the movie and popcorn, the two friends walked back home with Subbu having 10 rupees *in his pocket which would now go into his 'piggy' bank!*

Most people make money, spend and then save; but the wise make money, save and then spend. This is a much misunderstood statement, since many understand this as a *chicken and egg story*. Logically and mathematically both the equations in the title of this chapter should be the same. This is exactly where the human behavioural aspect comes into play.

Ever heard the saying 'Work expands to fill the available time?' Similarly, expenses expand to fill the available money. Therefore, even if you budget your expenses, unless you make savings as your first expenditure and allot money out of your income for it, more money will get spent than expected. Therefore we have to make a conscious effort not only of making a budget but also of sticking to it.

Firstly, let's learn to make a budget. This can be done in three simple steps.

Make a list of all the expense heads that you have or would like to have, including loan repayments and insurance premiums if any.

Trust your gut in terms of telling yourself which heads are truly important to you and which are not.

Write down the approximate expenses that would happen on a monthly basis under each head. If some of these are going to happen yearly, you may take the liberty to apportion them on a monthly basis or make separate budgets for each month. Such a 'month-wise' budget works out to be much better in the long run than a monthly apportioned budget as it gives you a more accurate saving target for each month. However, the first option sounds easier to start with.

Please refer to the sample budget sheet that has been provided in the next page.

Once you are done with these three simple steps, you may add the amounts to calculate the total expense (E) and then deduct this amount from the post-tax income (I) to get the savings amount (S). If this value is greater than 20% of 'I', you cross the first hurdle.

i.e. if $(S \div I) \times 100 >= 20\%$ ☺

If it isn't, then you may have to re-look at the expense heads and find out if any of the expense heads can be avoided so that the minimum savings ratio of 20% is achieved. If not, you have to worry about your income and seek measures to increase the same to bring the savings ratio (S/I) to this lower limit benchmark. If the savings ratio is greater than 20%, you may stick to that value.

And remember, as your income increases the savings ratio should increase as well, and may very well reach about 50-60% as you approach your retirement.

Now for the difficult part i.e. sticking to the planned budget. For salaried individuals, this can be accomplished with the simple trick of having two bank accounts. The first one would be the expense account to which your income first gets credited, and the second one, the savings account. As soon as the income gets credited in the expense account, you may transfer the targeted savings amount to the savings account. After this you may start spending from the expense account. This way your first outflow from the expense account would be your savings, followed by your other expense heads. Every time there is a revision in your income or at least once in a year, you may have to repeat this entire exercise.

For businessmen or independent professionals, this process becomes a little more difficult, as the timings of cash flows are not really predictable. A simple solution here could be to consider yourself as an employee of your business and fix a reasonable minimum amount as salary that goes into your expense account.

Keeping the business finances separate from personal finances is another very important mindset shift that this category of people must make. Generally their finances are in a huge mess with money coming in and going out into anything and everything; personal expenses going from business accounts, business expenses being paid for from personal accounts, additional capital requirement of business being funded by the personal money which rarely makes its way back to the personal account and so on. Fiscal discipline is most important here so that you don't end up investing only in your own business or profession without a parallel investment portfolio building up over a period of time. Own money always gets a step-motherly treatment than the bank's money. Therefore it is almost always good to do business with bank's money than ploughing back your own money into business. Your business is an asset and is quite possibly highly illiquid just like your real estate assets. Excessive investment of personal money into your business or real estate can lead you to a situation where you are rich in terms of assets but poor in terms of cash which is not a great situation to be in.

This doesn't mean that the budgeted amounts are carved in stone. Life demands you to make exceptions to your plans once in a while. However, the presence of a budget helps you by and large to ensure that the savings are on track.

Month-wise Budget Sheet

Cash Flow Head	Month 1	Month 2	Month 3	Yearly amount
Income	**1,00,000**	**1,00,000**	**1,50,000**	**14,00,000**
Salary	1,00,000	1,00,000	1,00,000	12,00,000
Bonus	0	0	50,000	2,00,000
Savings	**28,000**	**18,000**	**58,000**	**4,16,000**
Expenses	**72,000**	**82,000**	**92,000**	**9,84,000**
Food	10,000	10,000	10,000	1,20,000
Utilities	5,000	5,000	5,000	60,000
Self Maintenance	3,000	3,000	3,000	36,000
Pets	3,000	3,000	3,000	36,000
Celebrations	0	15,000	0	60,000
Entertainment & Outings	5,000	5,000	5,000	60,000
Health	4,000	4,000	4,000	48,000
Conveyance & Vehicle Maintenance	10,000	5,000	5,000	80,000
Insurance	0	0	25,000	1,00,000
Loan repayments	32,000	32,000	32,000	3,84,000
Savings Ratio (Savings/Income)	**28%**	**18%**	**39%**	**30%**

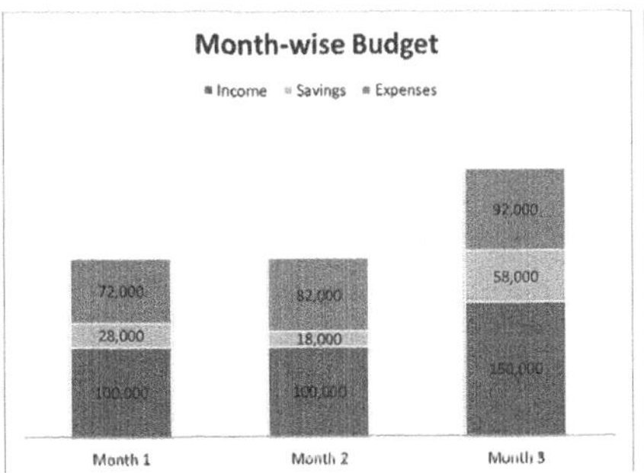

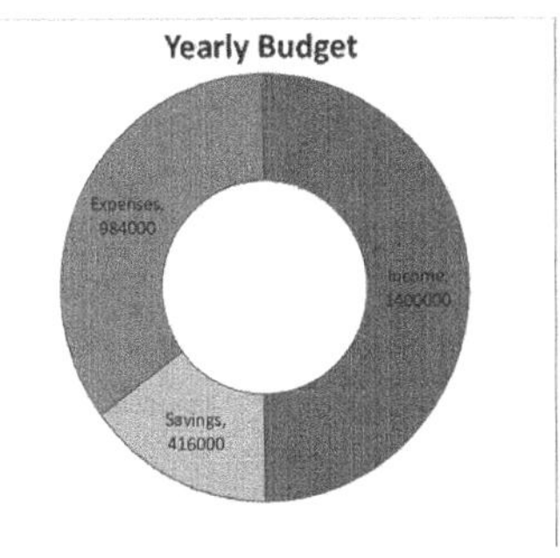

At a glance . . .

- ₹ *Wise people make money, save and then spend.*
- ₹ *Expenses expand to exhaust the available money.*
- ₹ *Make a budget and stick to it.*
- ₹ *Try to make a month-wise budget instead of a monthly budget.*
- ₹ *Maintain two bank accounts, an expense account and a savings account.*
- ₹ *Keep the business finances separate from personal finances.*

5

EMERGENCY AND PLANNED EMERGENCY

"Expect the best, plan for the worst, and prepare to be surprised."

– Dennis Waitley

Subbu's father was on his deathbed and he knew Subbu was a good for nothing fellow. So he left him a note before dying, which said, "In case you spend all your money and end up being a pauper after my death, hang yourself on the hook above my bed and die honourably, rather than beg on the streets." Subbu took this very casually and even upon his father's death continued living foolishly. Soon he squandered all his money and was quite deep in debt. He didn't know what to do and then he remembered his father's dying advice. 'No other option now,' he thought. He kept a stool on the bed, put a rope through the hook and made a noose around his neck and jumped down. Suddenly with the weight of his body, a door opened from the ceiling and bundles of currency notes fell on his head as he lay on the floor wondering if he was still alive or not! Did Subbu learn a hard life lesson? Will he live a financially prudent life, now that he has got a new lease of life? Only time will tell...

The first and foremost financial goal that anyone should be accomplishing is the creation of what we call as the Basic Liquidity Reserve. The amount of money to be kept in this reserve depends upon your current outflows including loan repayments and insurance premiums, if any. It also depends upon your current position in your career. The higher you grow in your career, the lesser your opportunities would be. Therefore, you may safely assume around 6 months' outflow as the reserve amount if you are in the lower to middle level management. For senior positions, an amount equivalent to 12 months of outflow is recommended. For businessmen too, a reserve of 12 months would be ideal as their cash flows are quite erratic in nature. However, I find them disagreeing with this aspect, as they keep needing money to invest back into business. If you are a businessman, I would like you to understand one thing. Emergencies don't strike you based on the nature of your income. Therefore it should be a part of your financial strategy to ensure that such a reserve fund is created.

Keeping one credit card handy with a reasonable credit limit also goes a long way in terms of handling emergencies.

We have to now understand the various types of emergencies that might strike you.

We can classify emergencies as 'natural' emergencies and 'artificial' emergencies. Natural emergencies could be anything that may 'emerge' out of the blue such as a medical emergency or loss of job. In such a traumatic scenario, the last thing you want to worry about is regarding money and regular expenses. And if you are prepared with adequate reserve amount, you will also gain a lot of courage to face the actual situation.

For example, in case you lose your job, the feeling of insecurity would increase day by day. I understand this feeling first hand as I was laid off from my first job during the dot com crash and was not in a very stable financial situation at that time. In such a situation the natural response is to find another job at any cost. You may apply some discretion but the pressure takes a toll on your judgement. This is exactly where the reserve fund helps you. Once you know that your next 6 months' outflows are taken care of, you would most likely treat the loss of job as a brief break from corporate life. With that attitude, your interviews would be stress-free and would most likely fetch you a much better opportunity than the one you had.

Let us now look at the same example in a different light. Say you don't like your current job due to a very rational reason that is out of your circle of influence. If you have the liquidity reserve in place and if you feel the market has the right opportunities for you, you may first put in your papers and during the notice period start looking for a suitable alternative. This is the way you may make use of the liquidity reserve to create an artificial emergency, in order to accelerate your career. However, utmost care and caution should be exercised while using this idea. Use it only when it is unavoidable.

Many companies now offer a sabbatical for a year or two in which people may try out their own venture. The liquidity reserve, if accumulated sufficiently to last the sabbatical period, may help you take advantage of this facility and take your shot at becoming an entrepreneur.

Most people start their careers at around 20 years of age and hope for their careers to last till they are 60. However, with the kind of stress and insecurity that is there at work these days, people get completely burnt out at around 45-50 years of age. Therefore, it really makes sense to take a conscious break of 6 months to one year to rest and rejuvenate at age 40, the mid-point. You may feel that doing so may relegate you in your career and your peers may go ahead of you. However, the converse may be true as you will be able to put more number of quality years at work if you take a conscious pit stop at 40. You may use this break year to also get your health back, by eating right, exercising regularly and getting the right amount of sleep and even getting a periodic body massage done. Not to mention the pleasure you could derive out of just lying around and reading peacefully a lot of books that you always wanted to read or catching up with all the movies you have been missing all these years. On a serious note, you may use this time to even upgrade your skill-set so that you become more valuable when you get back to work.

Emergency liquidity reserve is the starting point for all these to materialise. Therefore, the first thing you do once you exhaust this fund is to replenish it to the extent required and then get on with your other priorities.

I will close this chapter with what Mr. Hemant Deshpande, my client and a dear friend who today is an Executive Coach & Leadership Facilitator, had to say regarding his experience of making a conscious career shift.

"About 3.5 years back I was going through a mid-career crisis. On one side the work in the IT industry had become monotonous and stressful; whereas on the other side I wanted to pursue my passion. The real difficulty was - will quitting my job jeopardize my family commitments and goals? That's when I discussed with Chenthil and he worked out many scenarios for me to get a clear picture of my finances and how much time I had to generate reasonable income from my alternate career. It gave me tremendous clarity and confidence to pursue my dream career. Today I am slowly but surely establishing myself in my new career of Corporate training and Executive coaching."

At a glance . . .

- ₹ *The foremost financial goal for any family is to create an emergency reserve fund, also known as Basic Liquidity Reserve.*
- ₹ *Keep one credit card handy with a reasonable credit limit.*
- ₹ *Emergencies can be classified as natural and artificial ones.*
- ₹ *Take a conscious pit stop at age 40.*
- ₹ *Replenish the liquidity reserve once exhausted, as soon as possible.*

6

RETIREMENT – A LONGER AND LARGER EMERGENCY

"Don't simply retire from something; have something to retire to."
– *Harry Emerson Fosdick*

Why am I discussing retirement so early in this book? In a temporal sense, it should come at the very end. However, I consider retirement as nothing but an emergency! So let me continue from where I left in the last chapter. If the liquidity reserve was created for a short-term emergency, the retirement corpus needs to be created for a larger and long-term emergency. Does that mean you should stop working when you have enough of retirement corpus? Not at all. You don't accumulate the liquidity reserve amount to necessarily exhaust it. It gives you a choice whether to take a break or not and also protects you financially from any involuntary or unpleasant event. Similarly the retirement corpus is not accumulated for the purpose of exhausting it after a given period of time. It just gives you a choice of taking a longer break or changing your area of work. Probably something that you always wanted to do, but couldn't, because it wasn't remunerative enough to keep up your lifestyle. Or something that was totally non-remunerative such as a social cause, or was merely a hobby which you wanted to pursue just because you loved it.

For example, a client of mine had this beautiful idea of retirement in his mind. He wanted to visit different countries and stay there for a few months as a normal citizen does and experience their way of life every single year post-retirement. It was not only an expensive affair, but also something that couldn't be delayed to an age beyond regular retirement. Hence the retirement age had to be chosen based on his physical fitness and affordability. We conducted a detailed feasibility study and worked out an appropriate financial strategy which is being currently implemented so that his goal can be achieved.

Also, if the corpus is sufficient, any amount you earn after that is a bonus and will contribute in adding to your wealth.

However, in the unpleasant situation of losing your physical ability to perform due to health issues, the accumulated retirement corpus will help you to live a life of dignity and independence.

A few important pointers to be considered while computing the required retirement corpus are as follows:

The specific expenses that are expected to continue post-retirement need to be taken into account. Some expense heads such as those related to children and regular work may reduce, but at the same time, some other heads may get added. The more accurate the expense heads are, the more accurate the computation of corpus would be.

The timing of retirement is dependent on a lot of factors such as your lifestyle, current level of income, the annual growth that can be reasonably expected in your income, other liabilities and goals etc. This is what necessitates a thorough feasibility analysis of the various goals including retirement. This helps to find the most optimum time at which the retirement corpus can quite reasonably be accumulated. You may start with an arbitrary age of retirement, but then you may need to undergo a series of trials and errors to clearly pinpoint the time of retirement without majorly impacting the lifestyle and other important goals. (More on feasibility study and life cash flow analysis in a later section.)

Inflation plays a major role in the computation of retirement corpus. However, the common mistake while considering inflation is that it is done only till the time of retirement. Most of the retirement plans sold in the market do not even provide an inflation-linked pension post-retirement, leading to a simplistic calculation of the retirement corpus. For example, if today's expenses of a 30 year old are say 20,000 rupees a month, the inflation adjusted expenses at the time of retirement at the age of 50 would be say 80,000 rupees a month, the corpus required is calculated by simply dividing this amount by the monthly risk free interest rate, say 0.5%. This gives the corpus value to be 1.6 crore rupees. However, this amount does not take into account the effect of inflation post-retirement and the plan restricts the customer to limit his withdrawal to just 80,000 rupees per month once the pension starts. This means that say after 3 or 4 years post-retirement if the person wants to withdraw 1,00,000 rupees to adjust the effect of inflation, it is not allowed by the pension plan despite him having a lot of money in the account. I consider that to be the height of rigidity that necessitates the pensioner to reduce his expenses in real terms; i.e. from the perspective of the purchasing power of money.

Ideally the corpus calculated should be sufficient enough to overcome the effects of inflation even during the post-retirement phase of life and also should provide the person with an inflation- linked income. In the above example, considering the same inflation to continue post-retirement and say the life expectancy is around 80 years, (In this example, the inflation rate is 7.2% using the rule of 72. This rule is an approximate way to find out the annual rate of growth for a number to double in value in a certain number of years. For instance, if the expenses double every 10 years, the inflation rate is '72 ÷10,' i.e. 7.2%. For more accurate numbers, you may refer to the Expense Multiplier Matrix below for various inflation rates and number of years to retirement), and with the same risk-free interest rate, the required retirement corpus for an inflation-linked pension jumps to 3.2 crore rupees! This is double that of the previously calculated figure.

Expense Multiplier Matrix – For Projected Expense @ Retirement

Years to Retirement \ Inflation rate	0%	1%	2%	3%	4%	5%	6%	7%	8%	9%	10%	11%	12%	13%	14%	15%
1	1.00	1.01	1.02	1.03	1.04	1.05	1.06	1.07	1.08	1.09	1.10	1.11	1.12	1.13	1.14	1.15
2	1.00	1.02	1.04	1.06	1.08	1.10	1.12	1.14	1.17	1.19	1.21	1.23	1.25	1.28	1.30	1.32
3	1.00	1.03	1.06	1.09	1.12	1.16	1.19	1.23	1.26	1.30	1.33	1.37	1.40	1.44	1.48	1.52
4	1.00	1.04	1.08	1.13	1.17	1.22	1.26	1.31	1.36	1.41	1.46	1.52	1.57	1.63	1.69	1.75
5	1.00	1.05	1.10	1.16	1.22	1.28	1.34	1.40	1.47	1.54	1.61	1.69	1.76	1.84	1.93	2.01
6	1.00	1.06	1.13	1.19	1.27	1.34	1.42	1.50	1.59	1.68	1.77	1.87	1.97	2.08	2.19	2.31
7	1.00	1.07	1.15	1.23	1.32	1.41	1.50	1.61	1.71	1.83	1.95	2.08	2.21	2.35	2.50	2.66
8	1.00	1.08	1.17	1.27	1.37	1.48	1.59	1.72	1.85	1.99	2.14	2.30	2.48	2.66	2.85	3.06
9	1.00	1.09	1.20	1.30	1.42	1.55	1.69	1.84	2.00	2.17	2.36	2.56	2.77	3.00	3.25	3.52
10	1.00	1.10	1.22	1.34	1.48	1.63	1.79	1.97	2.16	2.37	2.59	2.84	3.11	3.39	3.71	4.05
11	1.00	1.12	1.24	1.38	1.54	1.71	1.90	2.10	2.33	2.58	2.85	3.15	3.48	3.84	4.23	4.65
12	1.00	1.13	1.27	1.43	1.60	1.80	2.01	2.25	2.52	2.81	3.14	3.50	3.90	4.33	4.82	5.35
13	1.00	1.14	1.29	1.47	1.67	1.89	2.13	2.41	2.72	3.07	3.45	3.88	4.36	4.90	5.49	6.15
14	1.00	1.15	1.32	1.51	1.73	1.98	2.26	2.58	2.94	3.34	3.80	4.31	4.89	5.53	6.26	7.08
15	1.00	1.16	1.35	1.56	1.80	2.08	2.40	2.76	3.17	3.64	4.18	4.78	5.47	6.25	7.14	8.14
16	1.00	1.17	1.37	1.60	1.87	2.18	2.54	2.95	3.43	3.97	4.59	5.31	6.13	7.07	8.14	9.36
17	1.00	1.18	1.40	1.65	1.95	2.29	2.69	3.16	3.70	4.33	5.05	5.90	6.87	7.99	9.28	10.76
18	1.00	1.20	1.43	1.70	2.03	2.41	2.85	3.38	4.00	4.72	5.56	6.54	7.69	9.02	10.58	12.38
19	1.00	1.21	1.46	1.75	2.11	2.53	3.03	3.62	4.32	5.14	6.12	7.26	8.61	10.20	12.06	14.23
20	1.00	1.22	1.49	1.81	2.19	2.65	3.21	3.87	4.66	5.60	6.73	8.06	9.65	11.52	13.74	16.37
21	1.00	1.23	1.52	1.86	2.28	2.79	3.40	4.14	5.03	6.11	7.40	8.95	10.80	13.02	15.67	18.82
22	1.00	1.24	1.55	1.92	2.37	2.93	3.60	4.43	5.44	6.66	8.14	9.93	12.10	14.71	17.86	21.64
23	1.00	1.26	1.58	1.97	2.46	3.07	3.82	4.74	5.87	7.26	8.95	11.03	13.55	16.63	20.36	24.89
24	1.00	1.27	1.61	2.03	2.56	3.23	4.05	5.07	6.34	7.91	9.85	12.24	15.18	18.79	23.21	28.63
25	1.00	1.28	1.64	2.09	2.67	3.39	4.29	5.43	6.85	8.62	10.83	13.59	17.00	21.23	26.46	32.92
26	1.00	1.30	1.67	2.16	2.77	3.56	4.55	5.81	7.40	9.40	11.92	15.08	19.04	23.99	30.17	37.86
27	1.00	1.31	1.71	2.22	2.88	3.73	4.82	6.21	7.99	10.25	13.11	16.74	21.32	27.11	34.39	43.54
28	1.00	1.32	1.74	2.29	3.00	3.92	5.11	6.65	8.63	11.17	14.42	18.58	23.88	30.63	39.20	50.07
29	1.00	1.33	1.78	2.36	3.12	4.12	5.42	7.11	9.32	12.17	15.86	20.62	26.75	34.62	44.69	57.58
30	1.00	1.35	1.81	2.43	3.24	4.32	5.74	7.61	10.06	13.27	17.45	22.89	29.96	39.12	50.95	66.21

The other mistake is to underestimate the quantum of inflation in the pre-retirement phase. The inflation rate that is generally followed is the WPI (Wholesale Price Index) or the CPI (Consumer Price Index). This only indicates the increase in price per unit of consumption. However, during the pre-retirement period, there will definitely be an element of increase in lifestyle and the number of units of consumption under various heads which renders the inflation rate in this period to be considerably higher than what is normally assumed. It would be safe to assume the normal inflation rate post-retirement as most people are likely to just maintain the same lifestyle and consumption in this phase. In the above example, if we consider an inflation rate of 9% p.a. in the pre-retirement phase, and keep everything else the same, the expenses at the time of retirement becomes 1,10,000 rupees instead of 80,000 and the required corpus further increases to 4.4 crore rupees.

Retirement is therefore the most complicated financial goal to plan for and the second most important goal after the provision of the basic liquidity reserve. All other goals lie somewhere in between in terms of priority and positioning. We will discuss more on those in one of the later chapters. We discussed planning the emergency of living too long in this chapter; in the next we shall discuss the impact of dying too young and how to handle the possibility of such a situation.

At a glance . . .

- ₹ *Retirement is an emergency – natural or artificial is your choice.*
- ₹ *Plan your retirement well to live a life of dignity and independence.*
- ₹ *Use the rule of 72 to approximately estimate the expenses at the time of retirement.*
- ₹ *Do not forget that inflation affects you in the post-retirement phase as well! Beware of retirement plans that don't consider this factor.*
- ₹ *Consider the effect of lifestyle increment in your assumed inflation rate.*

7

INSURANCE IS AN EXPENSE AND NOT AN INVESTMENT

"You don't buy life insurance because you are going to die, but because those you love are going to live."

– *Anonymous*

Continuing the emergency narrative, we can further classify emergencies as either temporary or permanent. For example, a fractured bone due to a freak accident would be a temporary emergency whereas the permanent loss of a limb in such an incident would qualify as a permanent emergency having a long-lasting impact on your family's financial health. We have seen how to tackle temporary emergencies earlier. However, permanent emergencies require a more elaborate mechanism to handle, and that is insurance.

The concept of insurance is quite interesting as it involves the entire society to provide protection for the less fortunate.

Therefore, it can even be argued that buying insurance is itself an act of philanthropy. Insurance works on the core principle of sharing of losses. Emergencies don't strike everyone at the same time as they are probabilistic in nature. This aspect is utilized by the insurance companies for projecting losses that might arise in a pool of insured population. This loss is divided among all the members of the pool along with a buffer amount to take care of various operational expenses and some profit and the same is charged as premium. In short, all the members of the insured pool get protection, while collectively contributing to compensate for the losses incurred by a few.

For example, let us say that there are a thousand people in the insurance pool and each one's life is insured for 10 lakh rupees. Assuming that the death ratio is 2 per thousand, the total financial loss would amount to 20 lakh rupees. This gets divided among all the thousand members, therefore each member contributes just 2,000 rupees.

This illustration is purely for the purpose of understanding the concept. The actual calculations use advanced probability distributions and mathematical statistics for computing the probable losses. They, in turn, determine the premium based on a particular confidence level. Thus we can understand that essentially insurance premium is an expense that cumulatively compensates the affected parties during any given year.

However, the human behavioural aspect towards this expense made the insurance companies change their strategy. People thought, 'By and large nothing is going to happen to me as the probabilities are too small,' and hence avoided this expenditure. This way, people opting for such pure insurance were less in number, reducing the predictability of losses. This is because probability-based statistical predictions work effectively only when there are large numbers of independent risk exposure units. Insurance companies found a very creative way to tide over this problem: to modify insurance into an investment product by loading the investment component on to the basic premium that would generate returns. These returns would camouflage the cost of insurance as the policy holder would, over a long period of time, get more money than what he has paid. This turned out to be more profitable for the insurance companies as their earnings included part of the investment returns as well. Since then there have been so many variants of investment-oriented insurance plans hitting the market on a regular basis. Add to that the tax incentive, and bingo, you have a popular product with guaranteed sales!

However, once you understand that the cost of insurance is anyway deducted from the premium, though not transparently disclosed in all the insurance products, your comfort level of buying pure insurance products will increase substantially. A major threat in buying the traditional saving-based insurance products is that they are highly ineffective. You tend to get severely under-insured since the premium amount increases substantially with higher cover, owing to the higher investment component in them. And with the general attitude of people being that of just buying a policy for saving taxes, without any scientific calculation regarding the financial liability to be protected, it's but natural that the sum assured (also called life cover) of the policies is quite low.

The second threat in these policies is that they are highly inefficient. Not only in terms of the cover per unit of premium, but also in terms of the overall return generated. This is because, the expense ratio is set on the total premium received; which means the expenses form part of the investment amount as well, which is not small. A typical endowment policy gives away commissions to the agents to the tune of 30-40% of the total premium amount in the first year. Add to this other administrative costs and it puts a major dent on your money. The way insurance companies pull off this trick is by offering a guaranteed return on these policies. The guaranteed value may be very small and for the uninitiated, who are ignorant about the power of compounding over long periods of time, even a mere doubling of the invested amount over 20 years sounds alright. But this amounts to an annual return of only around 4% similar to a savings account in a bank. Most of the traditional insurance products have a similar performance record. But the sales talk of the agents and their motivation to earn high commissions get the job done.

Hence, my message to all of you is this: do not confuse insurance with investment.

However, what will you do with such policies that you already have with you? The answer is simple and straightforward: get rid of them! If you find it difficult to surrender those policies as it amounts to a huge cost, you may use the option of making the policies 'paid-up.' In this option, you stop paying further premiums and the policy accrues a maturity value equivalent to what it should be for the premiums that you have paid so far and shall be paid out on the original maturity date. If the policy hasn't yet acquired any surrender value, it's better to forget it and move on with your life. The agent may make a last-ditch effort to convince you to pay one or two more premiums so that the policy acquires a surrender value. But be rest assured that it is of no use whatsoever, and will only make you lose more money.

There are many who simply can't come to terms with the fact that they have made a bad investment decision and lost their money. The fact remains that the money put in so far has gone down the drain. However, they will still put more money into it, hoping to salvage the lost amount. This, in behavioural finance, is called the '***Sunk Cost Fallacy***' or putting good money after bad money to recover the bad money. We need to accept the fact that we do make bad decisions and the best response after a bad decision would be to accept it and cut the loss. In case of insurance policies, do ensure however, that fresh insurance policies in the purest form are purchased before surrendering the old and inefficient ones.

Now let us take a closer look at the various pure insurance covers that you would need in order to provide complete financial protection to your family.

Life Insurance – A pure term plan either equal to the lump-sum replacement of your active income calculated at a conservative discount rate or your current income multiplied by the number of active working years left will give you a realistic amount of life insurance. This approximation however assumes that the rate of growth in income in future years would be the same as the rate of return on the insurance proceeds upon investing the same. This may not be a fair assumption as the growth in your earning potential may be much higher if you constantly up-skill yourself. Another disadvantage in this method is that you may either end up being under-insured or over-insured in relation to your financial goals since we are not conducting any feasibility study of your goals based on your income while using this method. For example, a 35-year-old person with two children will have more goals to fulfil than another person of the same age with only one child. However, if their income is the same, the insurance coverage with this method will also come to be the same.

A more accurate measure would be to extract all your essential goals as explained in the next couple of chapters and find their present value at a suitable discount rate. An approximate value can be obtained by simply adding up the costs of all the essential goals in today's terms without applying any inflation. This method assumes that the inflation rate of the goals and discounting or the investment rate of return are the same, which is alright considering the fact that the insurance proceeds would be invested in absolutely risk-free investments. (Please refer to the table provided for a detailed and more accurate calculation of life insurance cover using the income multiplier method. All you have to do is to multiply your annual income with the appropriate value in the matrix matching your years to retirement and income growth rate values.)

While implementing this, please ensure that you buy enough cover to make the insurance company take you through an exhaustive medical check-up. This will clear the air as far as the authenticity of information being shared in the application form is concerned, thereby not leaving any room for rejection of claim unless you deliberately misrepresent any information.

Income Multiplier Matrix for Life Insurance Cover @6% p.a. risk free discount rate

Income Growth Rate / Years to Retirement	0%	1%	2%	3%	4%	5%	6%	7%	8%	9%	10%	11%	12%	13%	14%	15%
1	1.0	1.0	1.0	1.0	1.0	1.0	**1.0**	1.0	1.0	1.0	1.0	1.0	1.0	1.0	1.0	1.0
2	1.9	2.0	2.0	2.0	2.0	2.0	**2.0**	2.0	2.0	2.0	2.0	2.0	2.1	2.1	2.1	2.1
3	2.8	2.9	2.9	2.9	2.9	3.0	**3.0**	3.0	3.1	3.1	3.1	3.1	3.2	3.2	3.2	3.3
4	3.7	3.7	3.8	3.8	3.9	3.9	**4.0**	4.1	4.1	4.2	4.2	4.3	4.4	4.4	4.5	4.5
5	4.5	4.6	4.6	4.7	4.8	4.9	**5.0**	5.1	5.2	5.3	5.4	5.5	5.6	5.7	5.8	5.9
6	5.2	5.3	5.5	5.6	5.7	5.9	**6.0**	6.1	6.3	6.4	6.6	6.8	6.9	7.1	7.3	7.4
7	5.9	6.1	6.3	6.4	6.6	6.8	**7.0**	7.2	7.4	7.6	7.8	8.1	8.3	8.5	8.8	9.1
8	6.6	6.8	7.0	7.3	7.5	7.7	**8.0**	8.3	8.5	8.8	9.1	9.5	9.8	10.1	10.5	10.8
9	7.2	7.5	7.8	8.0	8.3	8.7	**9.0**	9.3	9.7	10.1	10.5	10.9	11.3	11.8	12.3	12.7
10	7.8	8.1	8.5	8.8	9.2	9.6	**10.0**	10.4	10.9	11.4	11.9	12.4	13.0	13.6	14.2	14.8
11	8.4	8.7	9.1	9.6	10.0	10.5	**11.0**	11.5	12.1	12.7	13.3	14.0	14.7	15.5	16.2	17.1
12	8.9	9.3	9.8	10.3	10.8	11.4	**12.0**	12.6	13.3	14.1	14.8	15.7	16.5	17.5	18.5	19.5
13	9.4	9.9	10.4	11.0	11.6	12.3	**13.0**	13.8	14.6	15.5	16.4	17.4	18.5	19.6	20.9	22.2
14	9.9	10.4	11.0	11.7	12.4	13.2	**14.0**	14.9	15.9	16.9	18.0	19.2	20.5	21.9	23.4	25.1
15	10.3	10.9	11.6	12.4	13.2	14.0	**15.0**	16.0	17.2	18.4	19.7	21.1	22.7	24.4	26.2	28.2
16	10.7	11.4	12.2	13.0	13.9	14.9	**16.0**	17.2	18.5	19.9	21.4	23.1	25.0	27.0	29.2	31.6
17	11.1	11.9	12.7	13.6	14.7	15.8	**17.0**	18.3	19.8	21.5	23.2	25.2	27.4	29.8	32.4	35.3
18	11.5	12.3	13.2	14.3	15.4	16.6	**18.0**	19.5	21.2	23.1	25.1	27.4	29.9	32.7	35.8	39.3
19	11.8	12.7	13.7	14.9	16.1	17.5	**19.0**	20.7	22.6	24.7	27.1	29.7	32.6	35.9	39.5	43.6
20	12.2	13.1	14.2	15.4	16.8	18.3	**20.0**	21.9	24.0	26.4	29.1	32.1	35.5	39.3	43.5	48.3
21	12.5	13.5	14.7	16.0	17.5	19.1	**21.0**	23.1	25.5	28.2	31.2	34.6	38.5	42.9	47.8	53.4
22	12.8	13.9	15.1	16.5	18.1	20.0	**22.0**	24.3	27.0	30.0	33.4	37.2	41.7	46.7	52.4	59.0
23	13.0	14.2	15.6	17.1	18.8	20.8	**23.0**	25.6	28.5	31.8	35.6	40.0	45.0	50.8	57.4	65.0
24	13.3	14.6	16.0	17.6	19.4	21.6	**24.0**	26.8	30.0	33.7	38.0	42.9	48.6	55.1	62.7	71.5
25	13.6	14.9	16.4	18.1	20.1	22.4	**25.0**	28.0	31.6	35.7	40.4	45.9	52.3	59.8	68.4	78.6
26	13.8	15.2	16.8	18.6	20.7	23.2	**26.0**	29.3	33.2	37.7	42.9	49.1	56.3	64.7	74.6	86.2
27	14.0	15.4	17.1	19.1	21.3	23.9	**27.0**	30.6	34.8	39.7	45.5	52.4	60.5	70.0	81.2	94.5
28	14.2	15.7	17.5	19.5	21.9	24.7	**28.0**	31.9	36.4	41.9	48.3	55.9	64.9	75.6	88.4	103.6
29	14.4	16.0	17.8	20.0	22.5	25.5	**29.0**	33.2	38.1	44.0	51.1	59.5	69.6	81.6	96.0	113.4
30	14.6	16.2	18.1	20.4	23.1	26.2	**30.0**	34.5	39.9	46.3	54.0	63.3	74.5	88.0	104.3	124.0

Accidental Disability Insurance – Death may not be the biggest emergency after all. A permanent disability can wreak havoc on the family's finances not only because the income gets disrupted but also because it may result in an increase in expenses. Therefore it is important to have adequate cover at least to the extent of 10 years of income.

Regular Health Insurance – This one as you may already know takes care of your hospital bills. A *family floater* cover is preferred as it covers the family under one policy. However it is better to take a separate policy for elderly people in the house or else the premium might be calculated on their age. Many of you may be covered by your employer but here is the caveat. Once you change your job, the cover becomes null and void. You may argue that the new employer may provide one too. But the key word is 'may.' What if they don't? Or what if you fall sick during the time gap between the old and new jobs? But the most important question is what if you develop some health condition over a period of time and, after you retire from your job there is no cover? A fresh cover at that point would come with many exclusion clauses and could quite possibly cost you a lot. And there is a possibility that you may be denied the cover too. So it really makes sense to run a health policy in parallel to the company-provided one. You may go for 5 or 10 lakh rupees worth of health insurance, irrespective of the cover offered by your company.

Critical Illness Cover – There are some really debilitating and life-threatening diseases that one could succumb to, which could render the person unable to work to earn money. There could be long breaks that may have to be taken, especially after a major surgery in order to recuperate. These would be periods with no income and all expenses continuing as before. It is for this contingency that a critical illness cover is recommended where, upon diagnosis of such a disease, a lump sum amount is provided to the family. Regular health insurance will take care of the hospital bills and this will provide for the regular expenses. The recommended amount is about 2-3 years of outflows, including loan repayments and other insurance premiums.

Property Insurance – Natural calamities can strike any time. And if you happen to live in a risk prone geographic zone, it is better that you purchase sufficient insurance cover to the extent of the cost of reconstruction of your properties. You may also include other perils such as fire and theft into this suitably. However, if you live in an apartment complex, it is better that the insurance is taken on the entire building by the housing society because if the apartments in the lower floors are not covered, the apartments in the higher floors cannot be rebuilt until the people in the lower floors come up with the money for reconstruction on their own. In addition, if the property is taken on loan, there are provisions by which a few months' loan repayments are covered, subject to certain conditions, in the event of loss of job.

Vehicle Insurance – This is an insurance that I have seen people do religiously, so not much needs to be said about this. However, one key issue to be mindful of is, if you buy a used car with several months left for its insurance renewal, it is important to either transfer the insurance also along with the ownership of the car or buy a fresh insurance if the older insurance is not getting transferred. Otherwise, you will not be given any claim due to the principle of insurable interest. In the former case, the earlier owner has purchased the insurance but is no longer the owner, therefore insurable interest does not exist.

Professional liability Insurance – Those of you who are involved in recognized professions such as medicine, law, etc., should not ignore this important insurance to protect yourselves against liability claims by your clients.

All of these insurances, if taken adequately, would amount to a sizeable expense every year. However, this should be a conscious budgeted expense that needs to be undertaken in the positive interest of the family's financial future. There are people who ask me, 'What will I get back from these insurances?' And my answer is when you pay these premiums, do so with a prayer to God that you shouldn't need to get anything back from these policies. And spare a moment to think about those families who would need the money from their insurances and feel happy that you could positively contribute to their financial well-being.

At a glance . . .

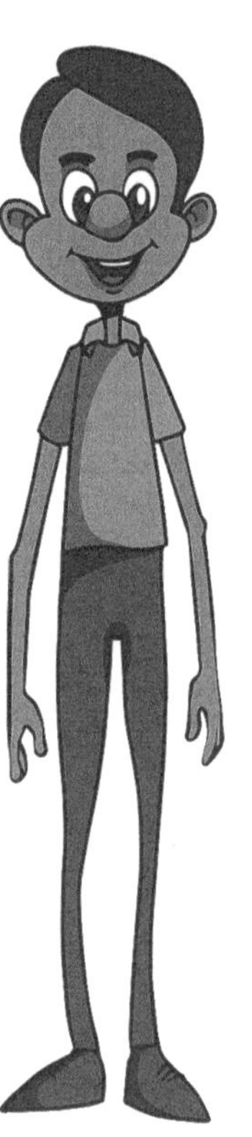

- ₹ *Emergencies can be further classified as either temporary or permanent.*
- ₹ *Buying insurance is an act of philanthropy.*
- ₹ *Cost of insurance is deducted from the premium amount in all types of policies.*
- ₹ *Traditional saving-based insurance products are ineffective as there is a high possibility of being under-insured.*
- ₹ *The high expense ratio in the saving-based insurance products results in the returns being below par.*
- ₹ *Do not confuse insurance with investment.*
- ₹ *Clean up your insurance portfolio by retaining only pure insurance products.*
- ₹ *Do not put good money after bad money. Escape the trap of the Sunk Cost Fallacy.*
- ₹ *While buying life insurance, ensure that the company takes you through a detailed medical check-up. Do not try to avoid it.*
- ₹ *Buy a critical illness cover in addition to your health insurance in order to cover the loss of income due to some major illness.*
- ₹ *Property insurance is best done by the apartment complex authority on the entire building.*
- ₹ *Remember to buy fresh insurance or transfer the existing insurance to your name if you happen to buy a used vehicle.*
- ₹ *Insurance should be a conscious budgeted expense. It is best to not get back anything from it.*

8

YOUR FINANCIAL GOALS – THINK BEYOND EMR

"Don't give up what you want most for what you want now."
– *Richard G. Scott*

We have always known this: if you don't set goals, you won't succeed. A lot of motivational talks happen around this subject. Those speakers most likely achieved their goals and became successful teaching the commoner why setting goals is so important.

The first question that we ask people when they go through our Financial Health Check-up service is whether they have clearly identified their financial goals. The options offered are 'yes,' 'no' or 'can't say.' We have rarely got a 'yes' as the answer. In fact, so many people, instead of ticking an option look up and say, 'We have a rough idea in our mind, but have never deliberated on it much.'

Do you find yourself in this category? If yes, you need a repeat of the pep talk. Else you can proceed to the next chapter.

Oh.. you are still here. Let me begin then. I will start with what the EMR goals are. EMR stands for Education, Marriage and Retirement. A large majority of the financial intermediary community thrives on promoting these emotional goals of a typical Indian. Undoubtedly, these are very important milestones, but it is important to think about living your life in a more planned way than arbitrarily spending on many other needs and luxuries that crop up on a day-to-day basis.

If EMR were the only major goals in life, it would turn out that you are earning money to raise your family, get them educated, get them married and retire. And why would your children earn? To raise their families, educate their children, get them married and retire. And the cycle repeats. Would you call this as 'living a financially fulfilling life' or are they just the routine aspects of your financial life?

Unless we write down our various financial goals, that are reasonably predictable in the future, we won't be able to figure out our priorities and allocate appropriate funds for them accordingly.

For example, we live in a world that requires us to have a car for our commuting needs. But this is not a one-time goal to have because once you get attuned to having a car, it becomes difficult to live without one. And one car cannot serve you for a lifetime. Therefore, you need to make provisions for regular upgrade or replacement of your car. Similarly, when you purchase a house, you also need to allow for renovation and repairs at regular intervals.

Other aspirations such as domestic and foreign vacations also need to be identified and their recurring nature needs to be decided and quantified. If you have senior citizens as dependents, a special medical emergency fund may be provided as part of self-insurance instead of blindly being dependent on insurance companies.

Your mind will keep getting influenced and swayed by the things that you see and hear every day. Those who wish to sell you something will always create a sense of urgency in you to buy it immediately. But you will be happy only when you spend your money on the most important things that you want in life and the most relevant at the time.

And that requires thorough deliberation and consent of the family members, especially the spouse, and ideally even children so that the plan has the buy-in of everyone and the whole family works as a team to execute it over the available time frame. Therefore, plotting the goals across the time axis becomes the logical second step after listing down all of your goals. A simple tool called the timeline can be used for plotting the various goals across time. A sample timeline is provided below.

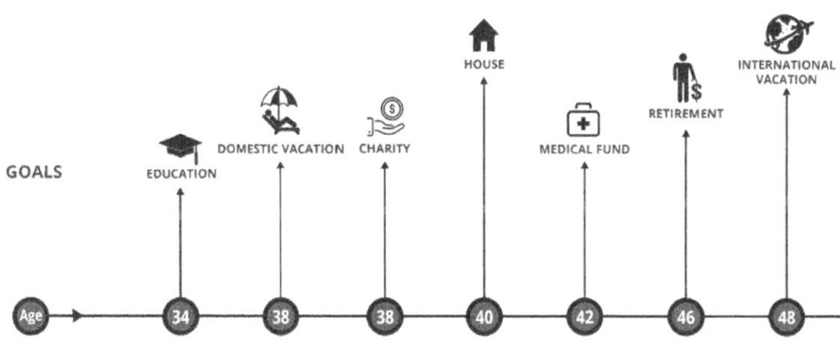

The next step is to quantify the goals and put the appropriate amounts against each goal in the respective year. Care needs to be taken to adjust the goal amounts for inflation, and in case some goal needs to be implemented through a loan, such as purchase of a house or a commercial property, the inflated future expense requires to be broken down into the down payment amount and the resulting repayment instalment figures. For simplicity you may consider these as yearly amounts. These numbers may be plotted on an excel sheet with each row representing a year and each column representing a goal. This would be the two dimensional version of the timeline discussed earlier. A sample goals calendar that reflects the goal amounts in today's terms and future terms is given below.

A Sample Goals Calendar

Goals / Age	Education (Inflation 10% p.a)		Domestic Vacation (Inflation 10% p.a)		House (Inflation 12% p.a)		
	Present Cost	Future Cost	Present Cost	Future Cost	Present Cost	Future Cost (Down Payment- 20%)	Yearly Instalments (10 years Loan)
30							
31							
32							
33							
34	100,000	146,410					
35	100,000	161,051					
36	100,000	177,156					
37	100,000	194,872					
38			200,000	428,718			
39							
40					50,00,000	31,05,848	
41							18,88,491
42			200,000	627,686			18,88,491
43							18,88,491
44							18,88,491
45							18,88,491
46			200,000	918,995			18,88,491
47							18,88,491
48							18,88,491
49							18,88,491
50							18,88,491

Again it doesn't mean that the goals cannot be changed midway. Situations change, priorities change and that is the most fun part of money. From time to time, money can be diverted towards the fulfillment of the most relevant goal without any compulsion for it to be spent on a specific goal. That is what a periodic review can help with. In case you didn't happen to spend a particular sum of money earmarked for a particular purpose in a particular year, you may either postpone the goal to another year or even remove it altogether from the list so that more money becomes available for another goal of higher priority. Alternatively, if you feel at the time of implementing the goal that more money than planned may be required, you may channelize some excess funds for this goal and reduce the allocation for a lesser priority goal scheduled for the future.

The goal setting exercise can most likely be compared to the preparation of a blueprint prior to the actual construction of a building. Once the first print is ready, you may review it and if you feel certain changes need to be made, those can be applied. Multiple such reviews can happen before you finalize the plan and start the construction. But once the building is constructed, changing the plan is not only difficult but also expensive. Similarly, multiple scenarios of combinations of various financial goals can be seen during the goal setting and feasibility study process. These concepts are discussed in detail in a later chapter.

We need to understand that the deviation from a plan becomes possible only if a plan exists in the first place. There is a saying that if you don't know where you are going, you are already there - nowhere! Therefore, it is very important to make a list of financial goals, make a plan or roadmap to achieve them, and if required, be flexible enough to take detours from time to time as deemed fit.

At a glance . . .

- ₹ *Most people have a rough idea of their goals; so they generally achieve them 'rough'ly.*
- ₹ *Many goals that appear to be one-time expenses are in reality recurring expenses.*
- ₹ *You will be happy only when you spend your money on the most important things that you want in life and and the most relevant at the time.*
- ₹ *Use a timeline to plot your goals across time and then quantify them.*
- ₹ *Be aware that your goals will change midway and hence the need for a periodic review.*
- ₹ *The goal setting exercise is like the preparation of a blueprint.*
- ₹ *Deviation from a plan is possible only if a plan exists in the first place.*

9

THIS MONEY OR THAT MONEY? – A BEHAVIOURAL FLAW

"Money is like water and takes the shape of its container. Whether you drink from a round pot or a square jug, your thirst will be quenched."

– *Chenthil R. Iyer*

Subbu went to the market as per his mother's instructions. She had given him two 100 rupee notes and asked him to buy vegetables with one and fruits with the other. Midway to the market he turned back home terribly upset and confused. On reaching home, he shouted to his mother, 'Mom, I forgot, which 100 rupee note did you say was for the vegetables?'

If you think you don't behave in this kind of foolhardy manner, think again. Remember the time when you got that additional unexpected bonus? Did you get really exotic ideas about spending the bonus money, which you wouldn't have spent if it was your salary money? If the answer is yes, you have been a victim of what we call in behavioural finance as 'Mental Accounting.' This happens in two ways.

The first one, as mentioned above, is about weighing the same sum of money from different sources with different values, where one of the sources gets an exaggerated value which I prefer to call as 'sweat value.' The 'hard-earned' money becomes more valuable than the 'soft-earned' money. We can do another thought experiment despite the suspense having been broken already. Imagine you have just received your salary after a whole month's work. On the other hand, imagine you have received the same amount of money through a lottery. You have a high risk investment in front of you that can double your money in a month. Which source are you most likely to take money from in order to put into this investment? I hope you are getting the point. As with any behavioural flaw, it is difficult for anyone to accept this immediately. However, once you are able to come to terms with it, it is important to take appropriate corrective action. The secret is to look at, in a very objective manner, the avenues to spend or invest, instead of letting your decision get influenced by the nature or source of your income. This requires continuous conscious efforts and keen observation of one's own impulsive responses as and when the situations present themselves.

The second aspect of mental accounting is even more critical. This is about keeping different sums of money separately invested for various financial goals. Also, we tend to conclude that those goals for which we cannot afford to put money aside based on the current income, should be indefinitely postponed or cancelled as we have already exhausted our surplus on the higher priority goals. Of course the higher priority goals need to be given higher importance. However, there is no reason we should tag various goals with separate investments. This method is inefficient because we do so with the limited visibility of current cash flows. If we project the life cash flows, i.e. the current as well as projected incomes and expenses along with the various goals at their respective positions and find that they are achievable at a reasonable rate of return, then all that matters is that we invest our surplus in an appropriate investment portfolio that has the possibility of giving that return. This investment portfolio could be a mix of fixed and variable return investments that are preferably not locked in for a long period as it hurts the portfolio rebalancing exercise. We will discuss in detail about portfolio rebalancing in a later chapter.

Subbu got a pregnant cat home and built a nice cosy cage for her. He used to proudly show off the cat and the cage to guests and friends who visited his place. He also made it a point to invite his relatives and friends for this show-off on a regular basis! However, every guest was perplexed to note one thing; there were 6 doors to the cage, one big and the others small. Some of his guests asked him why it was so, to which he replied proudly, 'I am expecting 5 kittens. This way each one of them will have a door to come out and the big door is for the cat!'

Maintaining a single investment portfolio without any one-to-one correspondence between any investment and financial goal is what I call the *Open Portfolio Philosophy*. Let me explain this with an analogy. Say you have to move into a village for the rest of your life. You need water for various utilities such as washing, bathing, drinking, watering the plants etc. Just like what Subbu did for the cats, would you be digging multiple wells for generating the required amount of water? *Or would you dig just one well, from which you will extract the required amount of water from time to time to fulfil the various needs?* The answer is obvious and of common sense in nature. Just like water, money is flexible to be used for multiple purposes. Therefore, if you maintain one portfolio with the appropriate asset allocation or diversification across various investment asset classes, it would be sufficient to fulfil the monetary needs as and when they arise. The only pre-condition is that we should be projecting the life cash flows and identifying which of the goals are achievable at a reasonable expectation of return. A sample of such a life cash flow analysis is given below.

A Sample Life Cash flow Calendar							
Year	Corpus @ beginning of the year	Fresh Income	Expenses	Net surplus	Goals due	Goal amounts due	Corpus @ end of the year with 10% return
2011	-	7,00,000	3,00,000	4,00,000	Nil	-	4,00,000
2012	4,00,000	7,63,000	3,24,000	4,39,000	Nil		8,79,000
2013	8,79,000	8,31,670	3,49,920	4,81,750	Nil		14,48,650
2014	14,48,650	9,06,520	3,77,914	5,28,607	Car	4,76,406	15,98,075
2015	15,98,075	9,88,107	4,08,147	5,79,960			23,37,843
2016	23,37,843	10,77,037	4,40,798	6,36,238	Trip to Disneyland	6,69,113	24,71,841
2017	24,71,841	11,73,970	8,63,447	3,10,523	Down payment for flat	7,93,437	21,56,767
2018	21,56,767	12,79,627	5,14,147	3,78,095	Yearly instalments for flat	3,87,385	27,50,539
2019	27,50,539	13,94,794	5,55,279	4,52,130	(Adjusted against fresh income)	3,87,385	34,77,723
2020	34,77,723	15,20,325	5,99,701	5,33,239		3,87,385	43,58,735
2021	43,58,735	16,57,155	6,47,677	6,22,092		3,87,385	54,16,700
2022	54,16,700	18,06,298	6,99,492	7,19,422		3,87,385	66,77,793
2023	66,77,793	19,68,865	7,55,451	8,26,030		3,87,385	81,71,601
2024	81,71,601	21,46,063	8,15,887	9,42,791		3,87,385	99,31,553
2025	99,31,553	23,39,209	8,81,158	10,70,666		3,87,385	1,19,95,374
2026	1,19,95,374	25,49,738	9,51,651	12,10,702	Son's education	47,58,254	91,71,535
2027	91,71,535	27,79,214	10,27,783	17,51,431			1,18,40,120
2028	1,18,40,120	30,29,343	11,10,005	19,19,338	Daughter's education	44,40,022	1,00,59,446
2029	1,00,59,446	33,01,984	11,98,806	21,03,178			1,31,68,569
2030	1,31,68,569	35,99,163	12,94,710	23,04,453			1,67,89,878
2031	1,67,89,878	39,23,088	13,98,287	25,24,800			2,09,93,667
2032	2,09,93,667	42,76,165	15,10,150	27,66,015			2,58,59,049
2033	2,58,59,049	46,61,020	16,30,962	30,30,058			3,14,75,012
2034	3,14,75,012	50,80,512	17,61,439	33,19,073	Daughter's marriage	30,71,524	3,45,62,910
2035	3,45,62,910	55,37,758	19,02,354	36,35,404			4,16,54,605
2036	4,16,54,605	-	-	-	Retirement	4,15,74,127	88,525

Also, special effort needs to be taken to ensure that the targeted saving ratio is achieved every year by sticking to the budgeted expenses, and the money invested in the open portfolio. Continuing the analogy above, this would be like fresh rains every year replenishing the ground water, thereby ensuring the availability of water for future needs. The only other variable in the case of the investment portfolio is that an intrinsic growth also happens in the form of investment returns.

Another important flaw in separately investing for different goals is the emotional attachment that is created with the investments, such as 'I will not touch this money as it is kept for my son's education.' This emotional attachment prevents us from getting out of bad investments and moving the money to better avenues from time to time. Also, if a particular goal that is due currently, requires a bit of excess funds for execution, this kind of emotional entanglement prevents us from using the available money earmarked for other goals to complete this urgent goal. Understand that I am not undermining human emotions, but only reiterating the fact that financial decisions cannot be efficiently made, if they are taken on the basis of emotions. Objectivity and rationality need to be the drivers as far as financial decisions are concerned and it's possible only if we consciously develop the habit of keeping our emotions out of financial decisions.

At a glance . . .

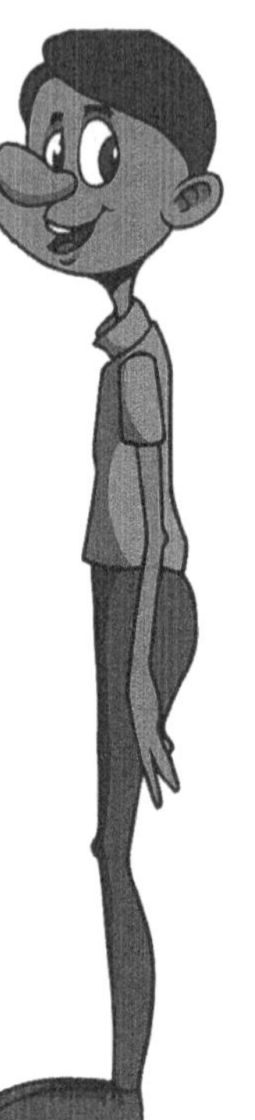

- ₹ *We have all been victims of 'Mental Accounting' at some stage in life.*
- ₹ *We tend to give an exaggerated 'sweat value' to sources of income that involve our direct efforts.*
- ₹ *Learn to look at in a very objective manner the avenues to spend or invest.*
- ₹ *'Open Portfolio Philosophy' is the art of maintaining a single investment portfolio with the appropriate asset allocation and without any one-to-one correspondence between an investment and a financial goal.*
- ₹ *Being emotional about goals is ok; being emotional with investments is not.*
- ₹ *Emotional attachment prevents us from getting out of bad investments.*

10

FINANCIAL STRATEGY – DERIVING THE REAL VARIABLE

"In strategy it is important to see distant things as if they were close and to take a distanced view of close things."

– Miyamoto Musashi

In one of the previous chapters we saw that the savings amount for any given year can be calculated as S = I – E. Once the expenses are optimized, it gives us a realistic target for savings during the year. So long as the income and expenses are fixed for the year, the targeted savings amount remains constant. Therefore, how much to invest is actually not a variable. However, many people try to derive how much to invest towards a particular goal 'assuming' a particular rate of return. This is totally counter intuitive.

Let me explain with an example. Say you have an annual surplus of 3 lakh rupees and have to plan for a total of 3 financial goals: A, B and C. Assuming a 12% p.a. return on investment, let's take two scenarios: scenario 1 in which the total required investments for the goals add up to 4.5 lakh rupees and scenario 2 in which the total required investments add up to 2 lakh rupees. In both the cases, we know that the investible surplus available is 3 lakh rupees. And in both the scenarios there are unanswered questions. In the first, where will we bring the additional 1.5 lakh rupees from for the fulfilment of goals? And in the second, what will we do with the surplus 1 lakh rupees available? In short, a lot of unnecessary effort goes into deriving the constant. A lot of online calculators provided by various product manufacturers use this as they have a limited scope of selling you an investment product. However, when we do holistic financial planning, it is important for us to consider these aspects.

At this point I would like to draw your attention to the previous chapter, where we learnt why we should be looking at creating an open portfolio rather than connect each goal with an investment product or instrument. Also we spoke about plotting the life cash flows to find out the feasibility of goals at a reasonable rate of return. This reasonable rate of return is the real variable that we need to derive based on the cash flows and goals instead of making an assumption without any logic.

Again, I shall provide an analogy for you to better understand this concept. In a one-day cricket match, if the target for the team batting second is 300 runs in 50 overs, we know that the team's required run rate is 6 runs per over in order to reach the target and win the game. However, if a team assumes a run rate of 4 runs per over and bats accordingly, they are sure to lose the game. Alternatively, if they bat super aggressively and try to score over 10 runs per over, they are taking unnecessary risk of losing wickets, which again may lead to losing the game. Therefore, the correct strategy to win this game would be to show sufficient aggression as required to score 6 runs per over and monitor the situation over by over and take appropriate corrective action on a continuous basis.

Similarly, if you are able to derive the required rate of return per annum in order to reach your financial goals and if you find this rate to be within reasonable limits, you are well on your way to accomplishing all your financial goals.

Further, the required run rate of 6 runs per over does not in any way mean that the team will try and score exactly 6 runs every over. The required run rate only indicates the degree of aggression or conservatism that the team should be playing with. In short, it indicates the strategy that they should adopt. In the same way, if the derived expected return is 15% p.a., it doesn't mean that you should be scoring 15% return year-on-year, but that you need to have the asset allocation with the appropriate risk profile. Only then there is a higher probability that on an average the rate of return realized would be around 15%.

However, if the derived rate of return happens to be inconsistent with your risk profile or risk appetite, it is a clear signal that you may need to realign the goals. To be precise, if the derived rate requires the risk appetite to be more, then either you consciously decide to do so, or you may reduce your goals to suit your risk appetite. On the other hand, if the required risk profile is lower than your risk appetite, you may either look at sticking to the lower risk profile or include more goals to raise the required rate of return and, in turn, the risk profile appropriately.

In both the cases, there is a possibility of seeing multiple cash flow scenarios with various combinations of goals that lead to different required rates of return and an appropriate scenario can be finalized as per your comfort. Continuing the example taken at the beginning of this chapter, the fact that even after assuming the return to be 12% p.a, the total investment required was coming to 4.5 lakhs. This means that with the available surplus of 3 lakhs, unless the required rate of return is revised upwards, fulfilment of all the three goals A, B and C is not possible. The investor can hence look at various scenarios of combinations of A, B and C with varying amounts, time horizons and even the possibility of dropping one of the goals that is relatively less important. Alternatively, he may look at increasing his risk appetite and freeze the scenario with the higher required rate of return that will have the possibility of achieving all the goals as planned initially.

This way, the open portfolio philosophy helps individuals to conduct a thorough feasibility study of their goals to arrive at the most appropriate financial strategy and derive the real variable, the required rate of return.

At a glance . . .

- ₹ *How much to invest is NOT a variable!*
- ₹ *Do not assume the rate of return; derive it. That is the real variable.*
- ₹ *Deriving the required rate of return quantifies the degree of risk to be undertaken for fulfilment of goals and hence defines the overall financial strategy.*
- ₹ *If the derived rate of return is inconsistent with your risk appetite, you have the choice to re-align your financial goals or to revise your risk appetite.*
- ₹ *You may create multiple goal feasibility scenarios that will have different required rates of return and then stick to the most optimum scenario that gives you peace of mind and comfort.*

11

IMPLEMENTING AND REVISING THE FINANCIAL STRATEGY – ASSET ALLOCATION, PLAN REVIEW & PORTFOLIO REBALANCING

"An asset allocation plan is based on your personal circumstances, goals, time-horizon, and need and willingness to take risk."

– *Michael LeBoeuf*

The proof of the pudding is in the eating. Therefore, once you derive your required rate of return and thereby decide on your financial strategy, you need to implement it by appropriately investing your surplus in a carefully constructed portfolio across different asset classes. This is what is popularly known as Asset Allocation.

Each asset class has its own importance and relevance as per its response during various economic cycles. Equity as an asset class is on an upswing during the boom or growth phase of an economy, whereas precious metals tend to shine during an inflationary phase, and debt tends to outperform during the recession phase. Though there are no strict rules in the financial markets, it pays to spread your money across the asset classes. From a financial planning stand point, real estate generally doesn't feature in the asset allocation recommendation due to its bulky and highly illiquid nature.

The biggest challenge in asset allocation is to decide what proportion of the money should go into which asset class. The simplest way would be to distribute the available money equally across the principal four asset classes, viz. cash, debt, precious metals and equity. Another thumb rule that apparently even considers your life stage and is very popular is to put into equity a proportion equivalent to hundred minus your age and the rest into debt. This makes it simpler as only two asset classes feature in this method.

I personally don't follow thumb rules as I strongly believe that thumb rules are for illiterates and it gives them a shortcut that circumvents their ignorance. Harsh words probably, but the truth. Any strategy ceases to be a strategy when there is no target to shoot at. Therefore, thumb rules rule the roost when there is no personalized strategy.

As we saw earlier, your required rate of return should form the basis for the asset allocation. However, the proportions cannot be decided based on generalized perception of returns alone from various asset classes. The classic error that is committed here is to assume the stock market index's returns to decide the equity proportion. It needs to be clearly understood that any stock market index is just one portfolio of shares, and that too, with an arbitrary internal distribution based on their individual market capitalization and cannot be generalized for any other combination of stocks or equity mutual funds. Therefore, it becomes important to do the basic analysis of the instruments that you consider to invest into and take their historical risk and return parameters to decide the proportion in each asset class, in order that your expectation from the overall portfolio is matched up.

The key parameters to be considered are the average returns and the standard deviation which is also the measure of volatility. (We will discuss in detail regarding this in the next chapter). Mostly people make their choice based on only the past returns and not on the basis of the measure of volatility. Therefore, when you try to choose the instruments you wish to invest into, it would make sense to compare their 'risk adjusted return' parameter. The most important such measure is the 'Sharpe Ratio,' which considers the risk free return as well, along with the average return and standard deviation of the investment instrument. It is nothing but the ratio of incremental expectation of return of a particular instrument over and above the risk free return to its standard deviation.

The formula is as given below:

$$\text{Sharpe Ratio} = \frac{\text{Expected Return} - \text{Risk free return}}{\text{Standard Deviation}}$$

Similarly, several instruments in a particular asset class can be combined in suitable proportions to have an optimum Sharpe ratio.

Further, it is important to note that the different asset classes can be combined in various proportions to yield the same required rate of return. It would therefore make more sense to choose the combination that would yield the minimum standard deviation for a given amount of return.

You may be thinking, 'It sounds very difficult. I better stick with my thumb rules.' That is fine but a little bit of effort on your part to understand the details will help you go a long way into ensuring that your asset allocation is more effective and efficient.

To give you an analogy, if you wish to create a garden in your backyard or terrace, it can be done in a very arbitrary way or you can do some study as to which kind of plants need what amount of sunshine, water, etc., and accordingly do the placement of those plants. What do you think will be more effective?

Once the asset allocation is implemented, the portfolio should be left alone for some time before we analyse it. Taking the gardening analogy further, it takes some time for the seeds to grow into plants and the plants to give flowers. Whether your strategy is working or not can be observed only after a period of time passes. I personally recommend a period of one to two years before which you may not disturb the portfolio in any way, other than in case of any extreme circumstance.

However, financial planning cannot be a one-time exercise and will be quite incomplete without a periodic review. A dispassionate and objective review helps in identifying what went wrong, what needs to be corrected, etc. Also, a bit of introspection about having put a genuine effort in the execution of the plan will go a long way!

As we understand that financial planning involves a number of assumptions such as expected increase in income, expected annual bonus, etc., and these assumptions need to be corrected from time to time, preferably every year, and its impact considered in the financial strategy. Also based on what pans out over this period in the investment environment, adjustments have to be made in the investment portfolio as well.

The Open Portfolio architecture helps us to do both of these in a seamless manner, the reason being the non-rigid connection between the investment instruments and the goals. All you have to do at the time of this periodic review is to repeat the cash flow analysis incorporating the required changes in assumptions and the actual portfolio value at the end of the year and re-derive the required return. In case the portfolio hasn't performed according to expectations or if the expected amount of fresh savings could not be realized, it would show as a higher required return for the future years and vice versa.

Bringing back the cricket analogy that we discussed in the last chapter, if the team scores just 20 runs in the first 10 overs when the required rate was 6 runs per over, it would turn out that they need to score 280 more in the next 40 overs. This brings the required run rate to 7 runs per over, increasing the risk profile of the game. Alternatively, if the team scores 100 runs in the first 10 overs, the required run rate falls to just 5 runs per over, reducing the risk profile.

Similarly, based on the revised expected return the asset allocation would require to be modified, and hence its risk profile. This is what we call as rebalancing of the investment portfolio. It is a perfect logical fit based on the prevailing economic environment as well. Let me explain. Assume that the equity markets performed exceptionally well in the past year. This would mean that some correction is on the cards and it would make sense to book some profit. When you re-derive the required rate of return in this scenario, taking cognizance of the exceptional equity performance, it would turn out to be lesser than what it was in the previous year. Accordingly the aggression in the portfolio will also reduce and hence the equity exposure, ensuring that some profit gets booked. On the other hand, if equity had performed badly in the past year, this would have led to an increase in the required rate of return, hence indicating a higher equity exposure, prompting you to buy cheaper equity. Similar would be the case in the other asset classes as well. Thus we can see that the open portfolio philosophy not only helps us to derive the real variable, but also to create a cyclic financial planning process which when repeated helps us to do a periodic review and portfolio rebalancing as well.

At a glance . . .

- ₹ *Create your investment portfolio with appropriate asset allocation in accordance with the derived financial strategy; i.e. your required rate of return.*
- ₹ *Never underestimate any asset class. Each one has its own importance and relevance as per its response during various economic cycles.*
- ₹ *Real Estate is a bulky and illiquid asset class and may hamper the rebalancing of the investment portfolio upon review.*
- ₹ *The biggest challenge in asset allocation is to decide what proportion of the money should go into which asset class.*
- ₹ *Thumb rules are for illiterates!*
- ₹ *The proportions in asset allocation cannot be decided based on generalized perception of returns from various asset classes.*
- ₹ *Use 'Risk Adjusted Return' for performance comparison instead of just return or risk.*
- ₹ *Allow some time to pass after implementing your investment strategy.*
- ₹ *Financial planning is incomplete without a periodic review.*

12

DECODING RISK & FINANCIAL LOSS

"Your biggest financial loss is the money you never made."
– Chenthil R. Iyer

Risk is understood generally in a negative connotation and therefore quite naturally evokes negative emotions. However, it is only half the truth. Most of the money actually gets made through calculated risk-taking, and hence the other name of risk is opportunity.

Let's start with defining risk in the first place. Risk is the possibility of deviation from an otherwise reasonable expected outcome. The definition only talks about the possibility of 'deviation.' It could be a positive or negative deviation; which means the risk remains positive irrespective of the outcome being positive or negative. Let me illustrate with a very simple day-to-day example. The elevator in any building is 'expected' to halt at the same level as that of a particular floor. However, if it halts slightly above the floor level it will be considered as a deviation from the expected result. However, can this deviation be cancelled out if it stops slightly below on another floor? The answer is obvious. Both the deviations contribute positively to the volatility or risk of the elevator.

It would pay to understand how this volatility gets measured statistically. Though I don't want to make this book too technical, I strongly feel that it is important to know how this parameter is measured. The most widely accepted measure of volatility is standard deviation which was introduced to you in the previous chapter when we learnt about Sharpe ratio. In the above-mentioned elevator example, assuming the floor level to be zero, deviations are measured as positive or negative based on whether it stops above or below the floor level respectively. That is, if it stops 6 inches above one floor, it is measured as +6 and if it stops 4 inches below another floor, this is measured as -4. Many such deviations are taken and each of these are squared up, and as you know, the square of any number (positive or negative) is a positive number. Once each observed deviation is squared up, the average value of these squares is calculated. However, considering that the unit of deviation in the above case is inches, the average value so calculated will have its unit as $inches^2$ or inches squared. In order to bring this back to the basic unit of inches, its square root is taken and that value is called the standard deviation.

If we consider the deviations as d_1, d_2, d_3, d_4 etc., till d_n, the standard deviation would be given as:

$$\text{Standard Deviation } (\sigma) = \sqrt{\left\{\frac{d_1^2 + d_2^2 + d_3^2 + d_4^2 + \ldots d_n^2}{n}\right\}}$$

At this stage it would help to know about the broader classification of risk in the realm of finance viz. Pure risk & speculative risk. Pure risks are those that lead only to a financial loss, if invoked. For example, the loss of life of the earning member of a family will be an irretrievable emotional as well as financial loss. Another example could be of an earthquake razing a building or a short circuit causing fire in a factory. No one can possibly make a profit from such scenarios under normal circumstances. Speculative risks are those in which the result of the risk getting invoked can be a profit or a loss. The risk of investment falls in this category, especially in variable income instruments and business.

Most people do not start a business as it generally involves a very high investment and a lot of unpredictability in terms of achieving success. However, those who take that chance and succeed earn multi-fold of their investments, and if the business is structured right, produce ongoing passive income as well. There is a general tendency to link business success with luck and gambling. This is in very poor taste, as luck is just the realization of action followed by the positive side of risk.

Subbu was a highly religious and pious man. Every day he would spend hours praying to God asking for just one boon. That is to make him win a lottery. This incident is a prequel to his winning of the thousand rupees. Days and months passed without any positive result, and one day, God got frustrated and came in Subbu's dream and shouted at him. 'I can't make you win the lottery unless you go and buy a ticket.' This was how the whole lottery series of Subbu stories started.

Therefore, fortune favours the brave who step out and take calculated risks and can also take financial losses on their chin. Again, to clarify on the gambling part, in a pure gamble there is no calculation involved. It becomes a matter of mere chance like the tossing of an unbiased coin or throwing the dice. Unless you do enough to tilt the probability of winning to more than 50%, there is no point in taking such risks. For example, if you make an investment based on election results, the predictability factor comes down drastically, and if you bet on such events, you may be gambling with your money. Such gambles generally get cancelled out over a period of time, and do not create long-term wealth.

Coming back to taking financial losses on your chin, it is an important quality that you should have in order to be financially successful. That's because you will make mistakes. And you will learn from those mistakes, correct yourself and move on. However, it is important for us to learn about a behavioural pattern that we all share. We tend to get emotional about the money that is already in our wallet. And so if you lose the money that you have already earned, a special emotional pain is created in your heart. Surprisingly, the emotion is not so much with the money that has not come in yet. We never seem to be upset enough about the money that could have come in but didn't because of whatever reason. That is why people tend to be happy with all of their money being parked in bank FDs earning meagre returns, even when they know that they are losing on the real growth that they can achieve by deploying part of their investment into the equity market. They keep consoling themselves, 'I am a risk-averse investor, so I'm happy with what I am getting now. At least there is no mental tension. After all, a bird in hand is worth two in the bush.' Once they invest in equity, the possibility of loss creates tension, whereas not earning superlative return in equity doesn't create a similar tension even though the potential loss of 'not investing' in equity is much higher.

I am not saying that people should always be tensed or live their life in regret about lost opportunities. The issue is about the unnecessary emotional connection with financial loss. The willingness to take calculated risks cannot come until we overcome this emotional connection with the possible financial losses. To put it in a different way, this emotional connection or obsession with the money you have is what is keeping you from the money you can have.

Behavioural finance talks about ***Prospect Theory*** which says that people tend to associate a higher emotional value to a particular amount of loss than an equal amount of gain, that is, they are generally more unhappy about losing a particular sum of money than they are happy about making the same amount. *We all agree with the point that money saved is money earned. But we seldom tend to agree that money not earned is money lost.* Accepting this corollary will set you at ease with regard to money and reduce your emotional intensity towards its loss. In short, your increased level of comfort in accepting financial losses emanating out of taking calculated risks will open up new avenues of income or profit that will far outweigh the losses you might incur.

However, care needs to be taken to not swing to the other extreme. There are a lot of people who go for broke with some of their financial decisions. In risk management one of the biggest principles is not to undertake risks that are catastrophic in nature. Leveraged risk such as derivatives is an example of such catastrophic risks. Warren Buffet has famously called highly leveraged derivatives that are not backed up by equivalent assets as weapons of mass financial destruction.

Many of us use the phrase 'high risk - high return' to indicate the relationship between risk and return. This is a misnomer as high risk doesn't necessarily give you high return. However, the correct way to understand the connection between risk and return is that, if you want high return, you have no choice but to take high risk.

A diversified asset allocation that has been described in the previous chapter is the best way to contain risk in investments and limit financial losses. At the same time, it helps an individual to explore more possibilities of growing her investments. Further, various possibilities for hedging using futures and options may be used in order to contain the risk of an investment portfolio, the details of which are out of scope as far as this book is concerned. For managing pure risks, various insurance products are available which should be effectively and efficiently used as discussed in detail in a previous chapter.

At a glance . . .

- ₹ *The other name of risk is opportunity.*
- ₹ *Risk is the possibility of deviation from an otherwise reasonable expected outcome.*
- ₹ *The risk of investment falls in the category of speculative risk, i.e. the result of this risk getting invoked can be a profit or a loss.*
- ₹ *Luck is just the realization of action followed by the positive side of risk.*
- ₹ *Gambles generally get cancelled out over a period of time, and do not create long-term wealth.*
- ₹ *We tend to get more emotional about the money that is already in our wallet than the money that could have come in but did not.*
- ₹ *The emotional connection or obsession with the money you 'have' is what is keeping you from the money you 'can have!'*
- ₹ *Money saved is money earned; and money not earned is money lost!*
- ₹ *Never undertake risks that are catastrophic in nature.*
- ₹ *'High risk - high return' is a misnomer as high risk doesn't necessarily give you high return. However, if you want high return, you have no choice but to take high risk.*

13

ROI - RETURN ON INVESTMENT VS RETURN OF INVESTMENT

"There are more fools among buyers than among sellers."

– Ancient proverb

Subbu was once watching from the sidewalk a goatherd herding away his goats. Suddenly a goat stopped in front of Subbu and started pooping. The goatherd came near to push the goat forward, when Subbu stopped him and asked him, 'What are these small round seed-like things coming out of the goat?' The goatherd thought quickly and responded, 'These are goat seeds. If you plant them, they will grow into several goats!' Subbu was very excited and asked him, 'Can you give me some?' The goatherd replied, 'Of course, but at a cost. I will give you all these seeds for a hundred rupees.' Subbu gave him the money, got the droppings home and planted them. How he excitedly announced to the whole world about the herd of goats he will have in a few months!

Sellers almost always know a thing or two more than the buyers and hence the adage 'Caveat Emptor' or let the buyer beware. This is true especially if it is an investment product that is being sold. The widespread ignorance of people regarding financial matters has only added to the number of cases of mis-selling in the investment world. Day in and day out, 'get rich quick' schemes get launched targeting gullible individuals. This is where we need to apply our discretion and choose our investments after carefully considering all the risk factors.

The primary thing to understand here is the difference between simple returns and compounded returns. Human mind cannot differentiate between the two and therefore is one of the most common ways in which a layman gets fooled. Here's how a good friend of mine was sold an insurance policy that technically offered a 100% return on investment the very first year. It was an endowment policy offering a 5% guaranteed bonus on the amount of insurance or the 'sum assured.' If the sum assured was 10 lakhs and the tenure 20 years, the premium worked out to be approximately 50,000 rupees per annum. Here comes the sales pitch. If the policy guarantees 5% on the sum assured as bonus every year, by paying one premium he would earn a bonus of 50,000 rupees at the end of the year. 100% return on investment and that too, guaranteed. What's the catch here? First and foremost, the bonus amount is just 'added' to the policy and would be available only after 20 years. Therefore, the 50,000 rupees bonus is not today's value, but the value after 20 years. But unfortunately for a layman it doesn't make any difference. Just to give you the correct perspective, in order to create 50,000 rupees as returns in 20 years by investing money even in a fixed deposit earning 7% annual interest, you have to invest only 17,423.52 rupees!! If you work it the other way round, i.e. find out how much compounded returns per annum you would need to convert your 50,000 rupees premium to 1,00,000 rupees in 20 years (the sum of the principal and the bonus offered) using the rule of 72, it is a mere 3.6%, which is lower than the savings account rate of interest. The perception created is that of 100% return which is nothing but the simple return for the entire term of 20 years, whereas the actual realized return is only 3.6% p.a. Even in simple interest terms, the return is just 2,500 rupees per year which is 5% of 50,000 rupees. The story actually improves as and when you keep paying the future premiums as the holding period of those keep reducing and hence provide a marginally better return on investment, and towards the end of the tenure, the returns on those specific premiums skyrocket to as high as 100% for the last premium. However, if you consider the return on the entire 20 premiums, considering the overall time spent in the system, the compounded return works out to just around 6% p.a. For such calculations involving recurring payments, you may use the RATE function in excel. The only care you need to take while using this function is to ensure that you use opposite mathematical signs for the cash outflow (premiums) and the cash inflow (maturity value and other payouts). I prefer to use a negative sign for cash outflows and positive for cash inflows. In the above case, the formula will be:

=RATE(20,-50000,0,2000000,1,0)
(**nper**, **pmt**, pv, **fv**, type, guess)

Note that the 50,000 goes into the 'pmt' section in the formula.

Similarly, for calculation involving a single investment yielding a single future maturity value, you may use the same function; only that instead of putting the investment amount in pmt, you have to use 'pv.' For example, if you want to find the return you realized on a share after holding it for 5 years, you need to put the purchase value, say 1,500 rupees as a negative number in the pv section and the sale value, say 2,400 rupees in the fv section as given in the next page:

=RATE(5,0,-1500,2400,1,0)
(**nper**, **pmt**, pv, **fv**, type, guess)

The result for the above case is 9.86% p.a. compounding rate of return. For all practical purposes, compounding rate of return is the best possible way to assess the performance of any investment instrument. It takes into account the reinvestment possibility of the returns generated from it on a periodic basis and the most common periodicity used for computing returns across the globe is the annual mode. Therefore, the first security question you may ask, whenever a rate of return is mentioned as part of any investment opportunity for holding periods more than a year, is whether it is a return that is compounding on an annual basis or not. If you want to be doubly sure, ask them to give an example, and using either the rule of 72 or for better accuracy the RATE function in excel, verify the same.

I have seen many government and private bodies trying to take advantage of the ignorance of people regarding simple and compound interest while issuing their bonds. For instance, there was a promotion campaign of a bond claiming to offer 12% interest p.a. when the FD rates were around 8.5 - 9% p.a. The advertisement claimed to give 3,40,000 rupees after 20 years upon an investment of 1,00,000 rupees. On the face of it the claim was true as 12% of 1,00,000 is 12,000 rupees which if accumulated as simple interest would amount to 2,40,000 rupees in 20 years. Add to that the primary investment of 1,00,000 rupees and you get the maturity value of 3,40,000 rupees. However, the fact is that these interest amounts, if paid out every year to the holder of the bond, could be reinvested in the FDs and earn further interest for the rest of the bond tenure. This is actually an opportunity lost by the bond purchaser as the accumulated amount is paid only at the end of the tenure. If you verify this example with the RATE function and find out the compound interest equivalent for this cash flow, it would be as in the following page:

=RATE(20,0,-100000,340000,1,0)
(**nper**, **pmt**, pv, **fv**, type, guess)

And the answer is a mere 6.31%, which is about half of the original claim. But you can't blame anyone but your ignorance if you fall for this kind of tactic. Therefore, it is critical for everyone to know their actual return on investment before making investment decisions and not get carried away by tall claims, irrespective of who makes the claim!

Further, the moment someone starts offering a much better return in an investment instrument than the prevailing market rates, your mind should get extra alert and start getting more information about it. The first step in the risk mitigation process is to obtain maximum relevant information. No one, who is trying to sell you something, would like to project the investment opportunity as a risky one. For instance, a real estate agent would tell you the best aspects of a property that he is assigned to sell. An insurance agent is bound to show you the rosy parts of the plan he is trying to sell you. This may amount to cooking up of some facts such as the rent paid by the previous tenant, the price at which a similar property was sold in the recent past, indicative bonuses paid by the policy, etc., which may not be easily verifiable. There have been instances where the same property has been sold to several buyers and the various buyers entangled in a prolonged legal battle. Similar is the case with investments in the Alternative Asset Classes such as Art, Movies, etc. Great stories are woven around such assets from a sales pitch point of view, but the possibility of losing one's capital remains very high there. In some cases, the assets just don't have any takers and hence remain illiquid, which is similar to having lost the capital. This is why you have to realize that the return *of* your investment is much more important than the return *on* it.

There are new business ideas cropping up every day starting from rearing goats to leasing cars, and from growing trees of expensive timber to under-construction malls that would give you rentals even before the foundation is laid! Each of these ideas comes in a very attractive package with great amounts of optimism and zeal that create a make-believe world of becoming an instant millionaire.

'You don't have to do anything else other than investing your money. We will take care of the rest,' is the typical sales pitch. They make you feel like a king until your wallet is opened up. After that the onus is yours to follow up with them and find out what's happening with the money. The core issue in all these cases is a behavioural aspect that I call Excessive Return Orientation, where common sense takes a break and your heart just wants to believe in the story woven by the salesman.

Don't get me wrong. I am not against superlative returns. I am not against taking calculated risks either, as I have mentioned several times. However, we have to learn to identify those instances where there is a malicious intent of separating you from your money by luring you with superlative returns. We need to have the wisdom to understand the 'feasibility' and 'sustainability' of an investment idea before venturing into it.

Now for the magic word that mesmerizes most of you and teleports you into a different world altogether: *guarantee*. You may be thinking, 'There are indeed people offering guaranteed, out of the world returns. Then why should I take risk with my money? There is an MOU signed as well. So what else should I worry about?' My question to you is simple. Tomorrow if that person who is offering you a guaranteed return loses your money going after a high risk investment option, do you really think that MOU has any value? Do you have the necessary time and money to take the legal recourse and recover your money? A more important and simpler question is 'Can anyone offer guaranteed returns more than one's own net worth?' If no, can anyone afford to provide guaranteed returns to several people, so much so that one creates a long-term sustainable income for one's own survival over and above the guaranteed payout, without overshooting the upper limit of one's net worth?

If you think taking calculated risk with your own money is being stupid, then let me tell you what is worse; to let someone else take aggressive risk with your money and that too, without being transparent about it. Further, there are stringent regulations against offering a guaranteed return, especially when the investment is made in variable income instruments such as shares or precious metals. Despite that if you get into such so-called 'guaranteed return' deals, you know whom to blame for the loss of capital.

May be you are thinking that I am contradicting myself. In one of the previous chapters I had mentioned that you should be willing to take losses on your chin and now I am raising concerns about loss of capital. The simple explanation to this situation is that while I want you to develop the courage to take losses, I don't want you to be foolish with your new-found loss bearing capability. And for those who don't have the time for deliberating and researching on the various opportunities that come by, or are too lazy to work on them, I have only one thing to say:

If you can work 5-6 days every week to generate money, you better spend a few hours a month to manage it!

At a glance . . .

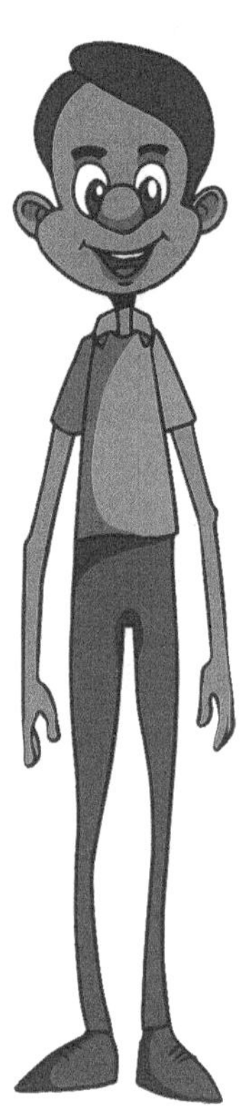

- ₹ *Sellers almost always know a thing or two more than the buyers.*
- ₹ *Choose your investments after carefully considering all the risk factors.*
- ₹ *Understand the difference between simple returns and compounded returns.*
- ₹ *Compounding rate of return is the best possible way to assess the performance of any investment instrument.*
- ₹ *The first step in the risk mitigation process is to obtain maximum relevant information.*
- ₹ *The return of your investment is much more important than the return on it.*
- ₹ *Beware of Excessive Return Orientation.*
- ₹ *Have the wisdom to understand the 'feasibility' and 'sustainability' of an investment idea before venturing into it.*
- ₹ *The most important question is 'Can anyone offer guaranteed returns more than one's own net worth?'*
- ₹ *To let someone else take aggressive risk with your money is what is called 'being foolish.'*
- ₹ *If you can work 5-6 days every week to generate money, you better spend a few hours a month to manage it.*

14

REAL FACTS ABOUT REAL ESTATE

"It's tangible, it's solid, it's beautiful. It's artistic, from my standpoint, and I just love real estate."

– Donald Trump

Long-term wealth, that too, something to be handed down from generation to generation has largely been created through real estate investments. This is one of the reasons why people get attracted to real estate. Moreover, as Trump says, it is tangible and solid too. These attributes give such comfort to people that they look at real estate as their first choice of investment.

Therefore, it is very important to understand the fundamental difference between financial planning and wealth creation. Financial planning is the process of appropriately investing our money for future needs and aspirations. Wealth comprises those investments that you do not intend to liquidate in your lifetime and would be your source of passive income in future. Therefore, the process of wealth creation should be undertaken only after having reasonably reassured the fulfilment of the various expense goals that one may have. This should be done as discussed before, through an exhaustive feasibility study, followed by adoption of an appropriate investment strategy and implemented through a well diversified portfolio of financial assets.

There are a few reasons why I don't recommend real estate to be a part of the asset allocation. This was briefly touched upon in a previous chapter, but we'll discuss it in detail here.

It may be beautiful, but is a bulky asset: Whether a residential or commercial property, or a simple plot of land, the value runs into lakhs or crores of rupees per unit and makes the asset allocation skewed unless your portfolio already is worth multiple crores. For a middle class family with a few thousand rupees of investible surplus every month, this would be impossible to purchase without a loan, incurring further interest costs. *In many cases the real estate asset becomes the proverbial camel in the tent leaving no room for any other investment to happen.*

It may be tangible, but is highly illiquid: How long does it take for you to purchase a real estate property? Unless you get carried away with the sales talk of the broker, from the time you first decide to look for a property, it should ideally take you a few months to complete the deal. Similarly, if you had to sell the property for some reason, it would at least take the same time if not longer.

It may be solid, but can't be broken up into small pieces: In most cases, a real estate property is a game of all or nothing. If you have an asset worth 25 lakhs and you need 2-3 lakhs for some reason, you may not get it from this asset. And it is highly unlikely that you will sell an asset worth 25 lakhs when you need only a couple of lakhs. This also makes it impossible for you to rebalance your portfolio, as it may require minor adjustments every year based on your revised required return.

The interest cost is 3-4 times the rental income received: Real estate is a much sought after asset class in developed countries as in most cases the asset pays for itself. The interest rates and the rental incomes are mostly in the range of 2-3% of the asset value and they mostly cancel out. Some developed countries have very restrictive laws that prevent anyone from buying properties easily. This creates a huge rental market and those residents who are eligible to purchase properties can put some cash as down payment and take the remaining on loan at very attractive interest rates. The rental income is more than sufficient to repay the EMIs and may sometimes put some extra cash in hand. And any inflation in rental income in future years will only help in repaying the loan faster or providing us with higher income. This means that most of the cost of the property is paid for by itself over a couple of decades, with us blocking just a fraction of the cost as down payment. Many of us influenced by the teachings of Robert Kiyosaki have ventured into real estate hoping to create passive income streams. However, the Indian scenario is much different. The IT boom has left the real estate prices soaring with rentals languishing in the range of 2-3% of the property value while housing loans are hovering around 8-9%. This means over and above the down payment, we have to pay the remaining cost of property over the next couple of decades along with 2-3 times the rental income additionally as interest. This drains the financial energy of people in their prime of life where there are several other priorities to be fulfilled.

No regulatory system was in place and there is no transparency: The property market in India was until recently highly unregulated and the prices quoted had no correspondence with the ready-reckoner rates issued by the government. The recently commissioned RERA or Real Estate Regulation Act is expected to bring in the much needed discipline in the real estate segment, but the impact of the same has to be waited and seen. Also, there is little transparency when it comes to the 'last traded price' of a unit in a particular location as there is still a considerable cash component in transactions. The recent demonetization drive has put a temporary halt on this but unless further drastic measures are taken in this sector, the required amount of transparency cannot be introduced. One such measure would be to let every property be broken down into small units and freely traded in an exchange, just like shares of a company. Real Estate Investment Trusts are a step forward in this direction, but they still are very rigid.

No intrinsic value addition: The growth in real estate is mostly the result of inflation in construction costs and the relative demand in each locality. There is no intrinsic value addition unless in the situation where a building goes for redevelopment, yielding extra space for existing owners. Even if one sells the property and makes profit and the money is reinvested in real estate itself, the new purchase also happens at the inflated price point, thereby reducing the effect of the realized profit.

Returns on real estate over the long term is quite meagre: At the dawn of the new millennium, long before the real estate boom started, a 1200-1300 square feet 3-Bedroom apartment was available in various major cities (other than Mumbai, of course) at about 15 Lakh rupees. Today, a similar property may easily cost upwards of 90 lakhs. This means that the property price has multiplied 6 times over a 16-year period. Therefore, the prices have doubled approximately every 6 years which results in a compounded annual growth rate of approximately 12% using the rule of 72. This would further deteriorate and settle around 10% for holding period in excess of 25 years. Add to that the rental yield of 2% and you get a long-term yield of approximately 12% p.a. which is quite average considering other asset classes such as equity, which doesn't have all of the disadvantages mentioned above.

Your house is not an asset: Most people live under the misconception that their own house is an asset they have created. In fact, it is a liability as it actually takes away money from their wallet for reasons mentioned above. You may be under the impression that you are saving on rentals but are paying four times of that as interest. Also, your house will get liquidated only to purchase another, thereby not giving you any profitability over time unless you reduce your lifestyle, after retirement, say by moving from a 3-bedroom apartment into a 1-bedroom or a rented apartment. These are highly unlikely situations and hence it would be safe not to assume one's house as part of the investment portfolio. Here I would like to share two contrasting case studies and will let you be the judge of which is a better and more logical approach.

The first case is that of a young couple who purchased a 4-bedroom apartment into which they were 'investing' 90% of their combined salary. Here's what they had to say when we met for the first time.

"We are newly married. But when we purchased the house, we did so with long-term planning. Today we may be only two. But soon we plan to have a child. When she grows up she would need a room. After 10 or 15 years, our parents will grow older and would most probably come to stay with us. They would need a room as well. At that time when we will have guests coming over, how can we not offer a room for them? And if we decide to buy a bigger house at that time, it will be much more expensive than what it is today."

Needless to say, they were living from hand to mouth with absolutely no possibility of investing in financial assets.

In contrast, here's what one of my clients did after thorough deliberation;

"In 2015, we were living in our own 2-bed room apartment. Then when I decided to start my new career, I felt the need for more space. Also our son was growing up and we, as a family, felt the need for a 3-bed room apartment. I did not have the funds to buy a bigger flat and that's when we discussed this with Chenthil. He suggested renting a bigger home. Initially, my wife and I

were not comfortable with the option solely because we grew up believing that we should have our own house. But when we looked at it closely, the option of renting out our apartment and staying on rent in a bigger house made a lot of sense. And that's what we did. We rented a nice, spacious, 3-bedroom apartment, thereby enjoying the luxury at a fractional cost of buying one. This was one of the best decisions we ever made."

Due to these reasons, it is better to consider any real estate acquisition to be a major financial goal intended for wealth creation and is accumulated only after checking for its feasibility with the help of the life cash flow analysis discussed earlier. Also care needs to be taken to ensure that the total real estate component excluding the place of residence should not exceed 50% of the overall portfolio. This would ensure the availability of sufficient financial assets at all times and prevent us from getting into what we call as the unfortunate situation of being asset-rich and cash-poor.

At a glance . . .

- ₹ *The tangibility factor of real estate investment makes it very lucrative.*
- ₹ *Real estate assets are bulky and hence resistant to being reshuffled across asset classes.*
- ₹ *Real estate assets are highly illiquid.*
- ₹ *Partial liquidation is rarely possible in real estate assets.*
- ₹ *The Indian financial environment is not conducive to hold large amounts of real estate owing to high interest rates.*
- ₹ *No effective regulation and lack of transparency make this asset class quite weak in the Indian context.*
- ₹ *The long-term historical return on real estate has been quite meagre.*
- ₹ *The house in which you live in is not an asset.*
- ₹ *Ensure that the total real estate component excluding the place of residence should not exceed 50% of the overall portfolio.*

15

WHY FEAR EQUITY WHEN YOUR INCOME DEPENDS ON IT?

"Risk comes from not knowing what you're doing."
– Warren Buffett

Whether you are a salaried employee, a professional or a businessman, the underlying source of your income is a business that is dealing with a particular product or service. This means that you have a stake in that business, directly or indirectly. And it is important for that business to generate profits regularly for your income to remain intact. However, one tends to take one's salary for granted and even is confident enough to take a 15 or 20 year loan to buy properties, assuming it would be repaid through the salary. A businessman is ready to take a loan against his fully paid-off home to fund his business. A doctor with a reasonably successful practice decides to grow from a small clinic, where she consults, to running a 20 or 50-

bed hospital on the basis of optimistic projections of growth in her number of patients.

The same people however, have an innate fear of investing their 'hard-earned' money in a successful and profitable company's shares. Why? This is mainly due to the human behavioural pattern where we tend to be more confident about what we know compared to what we don't know. And that makes it quite natural for a businessman, who is super-confident about his business and is quite optimistic about its success and growth, to worry about statistics of business successes and failures when it comes to investing in other businesses. In fact, in each of the above categories of people, their confidence arises out of their own capability of being productive rather than the underlying business itself. An employee is confident of doing his job well, and even if the current business that he is working for fails, he can always find a job with another business. His ability to perform remains intact. Same is the case with professionals. And a businessman will never think that his business could fail at any point in time so long as he is in control of it.

Therefore, it is important for us to address the root cause of this fear of equity investments. And the root cause of this fear is certainly not risk, as you are already taking adequate risk for earning your primary income, but the perception of risk due to little knowledge about equity. This is good news actually because if sufficient knowledge is obtained regarding this asset class, the fear and doubts can be ironed out which will enable each one of you to exploit the advantages of equity investments. Let's make an attempt to learn a bit more about equity here.

Contrary to many people's belief, equity investment is not a gamble. A lot of social conditioning also goes into creating such a belief system, some of which got handed down from the previous generation and much of which has come about due to the excessive influence of the 'trading' mindset being confused with investment. Trading in stocks aims at taking advantage of the price fluctuation that happens in the stock market due to the impact of various positive and negative sentiments. There are always two segments of people in the market: bulls, who think the prices would move up and bears, who think prices would go down. At any given point, the bulls buy and the bears sell, enabling a transaction to be completed in the market. However, these kinds of transactions are done with a limited time horizon in mind and are largely speculative in nature, without having the larger perspective of the fundamentals of the underlying business. This gives the illusion of equity markets to be equivalent to a casino where everyone goes and bets for or against the market and gets rewarded or punished based on luck.

Therefore, it is important to forget what you thought about equity so far and get information from a fresh perspective. Any equity share is a small piece of a business with the potential to bring home profits without the liability of participating in the losses of the business. You read it right. Common equity shares make you the partial owner of a company with a tremendous advantage. So long as the company is raking in profits, you get a portion of it but when the company makes losses, you don't have to partake in the losses. This works better than your own business or profession in more ways than one.

Firstly, the maximum loss that you have to bear is only in terms of the price you pay to buy the share because the minimum it can fall to is zero. Even this happens only in very extreme cases, and this risk too can be minimized by investing in a bouquet of high quality shares. However, in your own business, when you put in borrowed capital you become liable for the borrowed amount as well, through personal guarantees in addition to the capital that you put in. Secondly, you don't have to participate in the day to day decision-making. All of that would be done by a professional management team that works for and is accountable to you. For a smart person there is nothing better than this. Investing in the shares of a company can compound your time with as many employees as they have and also create a passive source of income for yourself through profit-sharing.

Thirdly, it is an open-ended instrument and does not have a fixed closure date. If the company goes through a bad phase and doesn't generate profits, you may sleep through this phase and when it emerges from it, you will start getting the profit share once again.

However, it is important that we do some due diligence before buying the shares of a company. To start with we may look at what we call as a blue-chip company which has been in existence for a reasonably long time and has shown substantial consistency in its business. Such companies may be slightly overvalued as their consistency and vintage command a premium. However, they would already be profit-making companies and would also be distributing handsome dividends year-on-year. These dividends are nothing but the profit share I was referring to earlier.

Here I would like to draw a comparison with a real estate property. I do not advocate comparisons between different asset classes but this one is purely to understand our own thought process towards investing and how our mind responds differently based on the circumstances. If you buy a residential property, you tend to get approximately 2-3% of its market value as rent in the Indian context. We can consider dividends from blue-chip shares to be in the similar range. Further, it is possible to invest the same amount of money as in the property in a diversified portfolio of shares across various businesses (sectors), thus reducing the risk of loss of capital. And if you were to buy a property for investment, and that too on loan, the same cash flow can be replicated by investing the equivalent down payment amount in shares and the EMI amount as Systematic Investment Plan (SIP) into equity mutual funds. You also have the advantage of immediate and partial liquidity in shares, which is not available in a real estate property as discussed in the previous chapter.

The biggest advantage of equity over real estate is that if the underlying companies continue to be profitable, the intrinsic value of the shares will increase thereby elevating their market prices in the long run, in addition to the demand-supply equation of the stocks in the market. There is no such intrinsic value increase in the case of real estate and it is always a demand-supply equation. Despite all of these advantages, people find it very difficult to hold equities for a long term and get tormented by the short-term fluctuations which 'transparently' reflect in the market unlike real estate.

I am not making a case for equity at the cost of real estate here. However, there are several aspects of equity that need to be carefully considered and understood which make it an important investment vehicle and an integral part of your overall investment portfolio. *If you can afford to hold real estate for over a couple of decades, then why not hold equity for at least half that time, ignoring the short-term fluctuations?*

A bit more research needs to be done, before you actually decide to invest in shares, than merely going by hearsay and recommendations of experts on TV. The balance sheets of various companies are freely available online and with a little effort you can start learning a few of the most important ratios such as return on equity, debt to equity, price-to-book, price-to-earnings, etc., and other parameters like net profit margin, sales growth, etc., and choose the best among the lot. Here I would recommend the book 'Romancing the Balance Sheet' by Dr. Anil Lamba whom I consider to be an authority on simplifying complex financial concepts for the common man.

Start small, gain confidence and then slowly increase your exposure to appropriate levels. And in the process, convert your trading mindset into investment mindset. Also never forget this: whether you are an employee, a professional or a businessman, you are already deeply entrenched in the risk factors of the equity world even without a direct participation through investments. Therefore, it would pay you better to learn about this market and participate in it than just get scared and stay away from it.

Greed and fear are two very important and relevant emotions that govern an individual's involvement in equity. Excess of either of the emotions would make one take too much risk than warranted or avoid risk completely. Therefore, it is critical that one learns to be sufficiently greedy in order that he doesn't exit a position with very insignificant profits; and to be sufficiently fearful to identify situations where the underlying stocks are considerably overvalued with respect to the fundamental parameters. This kind of a balanced view would ensure that one makes profits at appropriate times and patiently awaits good opportunities to enter the market again.

I have seen many people cringe when they, having made profits, see the stock price increase after their exit. A premature exit should definitely be a concern as the eagerness to book profits makes one forget to be sufficiently greedy. However, if the profits were booked after sufficient consideration and still one is worried that the stock price went further up only means one thing; the need to book extreme maximum profit. This thought process is the result of excessive greed as one doesn't want the other person who enabled his exit by buying the stock, to make any money.

Similarly, people who wait for a stock to come to its lowest point to purchase it are victims of extreme fear. They hate it if the stock price comes down even slightly after their entry and become quite jittery and impatient with themselves. Such people are never able to get themselves to enter into the market at all. It would pay one to be sufficiently fearful in terms of avoiding entry into a stock when the fundamental parameters suggest that it is overvalued or exiting a currently held position in such a situation without worrying about further growth. This kind of control over these emotions comes with sufficient experience in the stock market and with the understanding that greed and fear are not primarily negative emotions and both are necessary in sufficient quantities in order to benefit from the genuine opportunities presented by them.

At a glance . . .

- ₹ *The source of your income is an underlying business that is dealing with a particular product or service.*
- ₹ *The root cause of fear of equity investments is certainly not risk, but the perception of risk due to little knowledge about it.*
- ₹ *Contrary to many people's belief, equity investment is not a gamble.*
- ₹ *Any equity share is a small piece of a business with the potential to bring home profits without the liability of participating in the losses of the business.*
- ₹ *The biggest advantage of equity over real estate is that if the underlying companies continue to be profitable, the intrinsic value of the shares will increase, thereby elevating their market prices in the long run.*
- ₹ *If you can afford to hold real estate for over a couple of decades, then why not hold equity for at least half that time, ignoring the short- term fluctuations?*
- ₹ *It would pay you better to learn about the equity market and participate in it than just get scared and stay away from it.*
- ₹ *Excess of either of the emotions of greed and fear would make one to take too much risk than warranted or avoid risk completely.*

16

HOW TO INVEST IN EQUITY – STOCKS OR MUTUAL FUNDS?

"Genius is making complex ideas simple, not making simple ideas complex."
– ***Albert Einstein***

Equity is a simple idea of participating in a successful business and obtaining a share of its profit whenever it happens, and enjoying the growth in its intrinsic value over a period of time. In my opinion, the best way to participate in equity is to maintain a good portfolio of fundamentally strong companies' shares as mentioned in the previous chapter. However it would require you to inculcate the investment mindset and not be troubled by the temporary fluctuations that might happen in the equity market.

Subbu was waiting for a bus to go back home. Soon a couple of buses arrived; one was full of people and the other one empty. He had to go a long way and would have had to stand for quite some time before he got a seat if he boarded the crowded bus. So he wanted to board the empty bus but was confused seeing the other passengers get into the crowded one. 'Something must be wrong.' he thought to himself and boarded the crowded bus trusting the wisdom of the crowd. As the conductor signalled for the bus to leave, Subbu saw the destination board of the other bus through the window and found that it was also indeed headed towards his home albeit taking a different route. The bus had already started moving, but he wriggled through the crowd and somehow managed to jump out. But by then the other bus had left too. Subbu ran after it, but it was picking up speed. Finally he managed to catch hold of a bar and was about to jump in when he missed a step and was thrown off on to the ground. What started off as an effort to cash in on an opportunity ended up in the hospital with a few broken bones.

Once you make a decision to invest, you should be sticking to it as long as it is in sync with your investment objective. Sometimes it may so happen that after you have invested, another opportunity opens up which may look to be a better value for your money. The market is like an ocean, and opportunities are like waves. It is impossible to always ride the biggest wave or for that matter to ride all the waves. Trying to take advantage of all the opportunities will only make you spread yourself too thin. Therefore, it is better to enter into a captive portfolio of not more than 20 shares across various sectors (or industries) and market capitalisation (the total value of the free float shares of a particular company and is typically classified as large cap, mid cap. or small cap.) Also entering into stocks based on other people talking about it or buying into it, without using your common sense and doing your own research will only land you up being injured.

Once you identify a captive group of stocks and the appropriate prices to buy them, have the patience to wait for them to come near the target prices. There is a tendency in people to keep revising their target entry price upwards, along with the upward movement of the stocks and eventually, out of frustration, they end up buying it at the highest price. If you lose an opportunity, accept that you have lost it and wait for the next opportunity. Similarly, after the stock comes near your target price, if you panic seeing it going further down, you will never be able to buy into any stock. Therefore, clarity is important as to what the realistic price is at which you will be entering into various stocks.

Some smart-alecs try to bottom fish for stocks and in the process are not able to complete their allocation as the anchoring effect sets in. Let me explain this in detail. If the stock price reverses after bottoming out, one who is trying to bottom fish, i.e. to try and catch the bottom-most price of a stock at a given time, has that price set in his mind and keeps waiting for it to come back to it as his mind is anchored there. Even if it goes down as per his expectation, there may not be enough number of shares on offer at that price point. So it is very important for people to stick to the price point that they wish to enter and when it arrives, to enter wholeheartedly around that price. You should also be flexible enough to complete the allocation by keeping a 'target price range of entry' instead of a specific price point.

Do you know why Subbu couldn't become a gardener? Here's the story. Subbu wanted to grow a nice garden outside his home, and so went and bought a few seeds of different varieties of flowers. He planted them nicely at the patch that he had prepared. The next day he woke up early and rushed outside to see the flowers! But alas, there were none to be seen. He went to the patch and dug out a few seeds to see if they were really growing. He was disappointed that nothing much had happened. However, he planted them back and decided to wait for another day. Every day the same story repeated and then after a week, he decided, "This gardening thing doesn't work!"

Once you have entered the stocks successfully in their appropriate price ranges, it is very important to ensure that they get sufficient time to grow. Therefore, it is important to have two targets in mind. One, the target time horizon, which should definitely be more than a year, and the other, a target exit price, if possible to deduce from the various ratios that you have analyzed. The simplest of this could be a different price-to-book value multiple; if it is currently 3, you may choose to have the exit point pegged at a multiple of 4 or 5. The exit point would be the earlier of the two targets.

The reason I don't recommend people to hold stocks for more than 3 years as against the popular norm of 'buy and hold forever strategy' is because every company hits a plateau once in a while, and during this period, it may not provide the necessary growth that is expected out of equity. This renders the portfolio inefficient for a few years and in the long run could be devastating as you may get automatically sucked into their troughs as well, giving negative growth during such period. It would be better therefore to shift to a more efficient portfolio whose components are optimally priced with substantial growth potential based on strong fundamentals.

The main advantage of learning to manage a good equity portfolio is that it is an enjoyable activity and can be a 'stress-buster,' if you are able to take away your infatuation with money. It is as much a relaxing and engaging activity as gardening or playing golf. Again I am talking about 'investing' in stocks and not 'trading.' The easiest way to overcome the jitteriness while investing in stocks is to think, 'What will I do if this were someone else's money?' Automatically you become wiser.

The secondary advantage is that you save a lot of money in terms of the continuing management fees, intermediary commissions, operational expenses of the product manufacturer, etc., as applicable. There is only a one-time brokerage cost at the time of entry and exit whenever that may be. Even in that case, there are many service providers that work on a fixed cost basis that work out to be much cheaper when there are large volumes. There is no cost on just holding onto your investment unlike other products like equity mutual funds or PMS.

However, if you find all of these too difficult to implement, it is better to shell out some money directly or indirectly to the experts in the field, equity mutual funds being the next best way to enter the equity world. Quite possibly, this route would be less expensive than you making major mistakes trying to learn the tricks of the direct stocks environment. Some of you may even get disturbed due to the frequent fluctuations that happen in the markets. Moreover, if your primary income source takes away bulk of your time, it would be a good idea to incur some expenses in this regard and not act in a 'penny wise and pound foolish' manner.

At this juncture, it would help to know some of the disadvantages of the mutual fund route other than the exorbitant and continuing costs of management as a significant percentage of the fund value every year. Fund houses make investment decisions on behalf of lakhs of investors and therefore their trade sizes are bound to be huge. Therefore, any entry and exit of the fund house in the market will be inefficient in terms of having to buy higher or sell lower than the prevailing market rates. This happens because there may not be enough liquidity in the various scrips at a given point in time and so may have to keep buying from sellers offering to sell at higher prices to complete the mandate. Similarly, when they sell, buyers will be stacked in the opposite direction and therefore may have to keep selling at lower rates.

Further, since most of the equity mutual funds are open-ended, there is continuous inflow and outflow of money. However, if the net inflow is higher, the fund house has to deploy it at the prevailing market rates as per its mandate. Therefore, there is no question of waiting for the market or the individual stocks to correct for the purpose of deployment of fresh funds. On the other hand, if the redemptions are more than the inflows, there might arise a situation where the fund has to liquidate the underlying shares at the prevailing market value. Both these situations in fact increase the riskiness of the fund.

Also, most of the mutual funds are victims of over-diversification. Diversification, to a particular extent, helps in reducing the risk of extreme volatility that may happen in individual stocks. However, excessive diversification, where in some cases there is exposure to more than 40 or 50 companies, the value of diversification reduces. This is because it increases the possibility of getting hit due to volatility in any and every sector impacting performance adversely. The biblical story of David and Goliath explains this thoroughly. Goliath was a giant who constantly harassed the villagers but no one would stand up to fight him. Finally a small boy named David came forward to fight Goliath with his slingshot. The villagers mocked him and tried to tell him that he was a small boy and Goliath was too big for him to hit. The reply that David gave them is an absolute classic. He said, '*Goliath is not too big for me to hit; he is too big for me to miss!*' Many mutual funds have become too big for volatility to miss.

All of these effects, including that of the fund management charges, get absorbed in the calculation of their Net Asset Value or in short the NAV of the fund. This means that irrespective of when and with how much money you entered the fund, the behaviour and the investments of other investors in the pool, whether good or bad, affects the performance of your money. We can only hope that these positive and negative effects will neutralize each other over a period of time and provide you with appropriate performance.

From a cost-cutting point of view, there is definitely a new possibility that has been created; the 'direct plans' in mutual funds. These plans that are replicas of existing mutual fund schemes provide the same portfolio with enhanced performance due to a substantially less cost structure, by eliminating the commissions paid to the middle-men or agents.

If you are a small investor, and would like to test the waters in the equity markets with a few thousand rupees a month, I would definitely recommend the mutual fund route, and in such a scenario, there wouldn't be much of a difference between direct and regular plans. However, there is simply no point in entering mutual funds with large volumes of money as you can easily create a good direct stocks portfolio with that kind of money, keeping the right weight or proportion for each stock. To start with, you may even mirror the portfolios of established schemes which are openly available, saving tremendous amounts of cost. Even with a few lakhs rupees, you will be able to create a well-diversified and balanced equity portfolio.

The real value of equity mutual funds is for the small investors who may not be in a position to create such a portfolio with the limited money that they may have. This is because, creating a diversified portfolio of say 20 stocks with their prices ranging from a few rupees to a few thousand rupees per share would be impossible, keeping their respective proportions in the portfolio intact; i.e. without a sum of money that would be the least possible multiple of the highest priced share that can accommodate a whole number of each of the remaining shares.

For example, let's say we want to prepare a portfolio between 5 stocks A,B,C,D & E with their respective prices as 50, 200, 500, 1000 and 5000 per share. If the proportions of these in the portfolio are 20%, 30%, 10%, 35% and 5% respectively, we would need at least 1 lakh rupees to build this portfolio so that at least 1 share of stock E would form 5% of the portfolio. The remaining 95,000 would be distributed into A, B, C and D as 20,000 (forming 400 shares of A), 30,000 (forming 150 shares of B), 10,000 (forming 20 shares of C), and 35,000 (forming 35 shares of D) respectively. Imagine the amount required to accommodate 20 stocks in a portfolio with each having varied proportions.

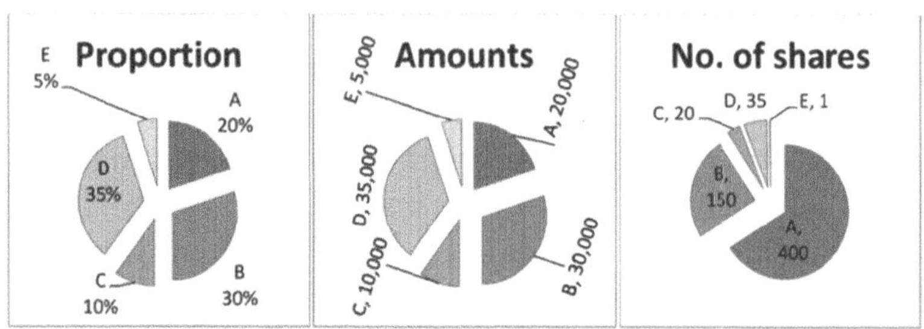

The process of selecting an equity mutual fund is much simpler than selecting direct stocks. A simple parameter, the 'sharpe ratio' as discussed in a previous chapter, would be helpful in selecting the fund with the best risk adjusted return in the diversified equity mutual fund category, the one having the largest sharpe ratio being the best. Sharpe ratio of the various mutual fund schemes would be readily available in the various financial portals and you may choose 2-3 schemes for accommodating the philosophies of multiple fund managers.

Regarding Initial Public Offerings (IPOs) and New Fund Offers (NFOs), my advice is in two words 'Avoid them.' When you are investing your hard-earned money in equity directly or through mutual funds, it is important that you look for consistency in their performance parameters. That would require the stock or fund to be available in the market for at least 3 years. The strategy is simple. Let the traders test the waters with their money, we shall enter later. The argument against this approach is generally about the opportunity lost in terms of capturing them at the lowest point, which is a myth.

An IPO gets priced based on the promoters' outlook about future opportunities certified by a merchant banker, and as in any other entrepreneur's case, it is bound to be biased. If they are so sure, why sell their equity? They could easily execute their foolproof plans through a loan at a much cheaper rate than diluting their stake. However, that is not the case. Companies floating IPOs are looking for liability-free money, and rightly so, as part of their growth strategy. In many cases, they are looking for giving an exit route to their early private equity investors. I am not attributing any negative motive here to those companies, but cautioning you not to jump into the bandwagon based on hearsay. And investing in an IPO with an intention of getting the early mover advantage is definitely not the right reason.

The way NFOs are sold is quite funny. The most popular storyline revolves around the 10 rupees NAV. Those who sell this idea either are parroting the sales talk that they have been taught without applying their mind or are deliberately trying to mis-sell. The truth of the matter is that irrespective of the NAV, the fresh money that you put in is going right into the underlying market, which is the same for any fund. So, there is literally no advantage of getting such a low NAV. The main differentiating factor could be the quality of the fund management, which however will be revealed only over a period of time. Moreover, the cost structure for an NFO is much higher than an established fund and so are the commissions. Got the point?

At a glance . . .

- ₹ *Once you make a decision to invest, you should be sticking to it as long as it is in sync with your investment objective.* 
- ₹ *The market is like an ocean, and opportunities are like waves.*
- ₹ *Clarity is important as to what is the realistic price at which you will be entering into various stocks.*
- ₹ *Keep a 'target price range of entry' instead of a specific price point.*
- ₹ *It is important to have two targets in mind once you enter stocks: the target time horizon and a target exit price.*
- ₹ *The easiest way to overcome the jitteriness while investing in stocks is to think, 'What will I do if this were someone else's money?'*
- ₹ *Managing a good equity portfolio is an enjoyable activity and can be a 'stress-buster,' if you take away your infatuation with money.*
- ₹ *Investments in a sound equity portfolio are devoid of any charges and fees on an on-going basis unlike other equity instruments.*
- ₹ *Equity mutual fund is the second best way to enter the equity world.*

- ₹ *Direct plans in equity mutual funds are replicas of existing schemes that provide the same portfolio with enhanced performance due to a substantially less cost structure.*
- ₹ *There is simply no point in entering mutual funds with large volumes of money as you can easily create a reasonably diversified and well balanced direct stocks portfolio with that kind of money.*
- ₹ *The real value of equity mutual funds is for the small investors who may not be in a position to create such a portfolio with the limited money that they may have.*
- ₹ *Avoid IPOs and NFOs as far as possible.*

17

DEBT MUTUAL FUNDS – FOR LONG-TERM DEBT INVESTMENT

"Compounding works continuously and predictably only in fixed income instruments, since future returns do not have the power to erode past returns as in every other case."

– Chenthil R. Iyer

Debt is commonly understood as loan, and rightly so. It is just that the one who takes the loan pays interest to the other person who is said to have invested in this loan! The most popular investment instrument, fixed deposit in a bank, is a loan that you give to the bank. Similarly, a time deposit or recurring deposit in the post office, public provident fund, Kisaan Vikas Patra, National Savings Certificate, Government Of India bonds, etc., are all different forms of loans taken by the government from public. Even private companies issue bonds, i.e. take loan from the public when they need cheaper loans to fund their various business activities. All of these are broadly classified as debt instruments.

Investment in debt brings in stability and predictability in cash flows unlike equity, and therefore plays an important role in the investment portfolio of an individual. Therefore, they are also called as fixed income instruments. The power of compounding works continuously only in these instruments as there is no possibility of future returns eroding the past returns, if these instruments are held till maturity. Does that mean that these instruments are risk-free? Not at all. There are a host of different risks that can influence the performance of these instruments. Some of the most important ones are discussed below.

Default Risk – This represents the possibility of the entity taking the loan not being able to repay the same. The default could either be in terms of not being able to adhere to the timelines of interest or principal payment, or in terms of the very payment of these amounts.

Reinvestment Risk – A debt instrument generally has a fixed maturity period and therefore, the capital coming out at that point needs to be reinvested. At the time of reinvestment, the rate of interest on a similar debt instrument could be different from what was in the previous one, for the better or worse, and hence the risk.

Interest Rate Risk – This arises when someone needs liquidity during the tenure of the instrument. The interest or coupon payment in a debt instrument does not vary till its maturity. However, the general interest rates in the market could fluctuate based on the central bank's monetary policies. This fluctuation impacts the value of these instruments in the secondary market. For instance, if the interest rate increases, why would someone buy into your instrument that offers a lower interest at the actual value? This factor creates a dent in the price of the instrument. The situation gets reversed if the interest rates fall and the instrument gets traded off at a premium. Those who wish to exit the instrument in the middle of the regular tenure have to be mindful of this factor.

Just like stocks, it is important to create a diversified portfolio of debt instruments. The variables could be the remaining maturity period, the credit worthiness of the debt paper, coupon rate (though the interest rate fluctuations are absorbed in the bond price, how fast the money comes out of the instrument is also an important parameter measured as 'duration.' The higher the coupon rate, the lesser the duration, and this is considered to be better), the nature of the debt instrument (coupon bearing/cumulative or tradable/non-tradable), and its type (sovereign security or private).

Unlike in stocks, I would not recommend you to directly hold a portfolio of debt instruments for various reasons mentioned below. Instead, it would be a very good idea to hold 2-3 debt mutual funds.

Low Management Cost – The costs are substantially lower and for this very reason most of the agents do not sell these funds. Most people that I have interacted with were aware of equity mutual funds but they were totally ignorant about debt mutual funds. This only goes to show that not enough has been done to promote debt funds to the public at large. The advent of direct plans has only helped to reduce this cost further.

Managing Maturities – This is a big pain point while handling a debt portfolio. As the papers have a fixed maturity period, the money that comes out needs to be reinvested appropriately into other securities and that too, according to the proportions of papers required of different tenures in the portfolio. This is because some of the papers which qualified as long-term in the beginning would have become short-term upon the maturity of the originally short-term papers. A lot of time and effort goes into this which is best outsourced to a fund manager.

Better Taxation Norms – This is quite interesting. If you hold the debt instruments such as fixed deposits, bonds, etc., directly, the interest income falls under the head, 'income from other sources' and gets taxed at marginal rates, and that too, on a year-on-year basis. For those in the 20% tax bracket and above, it turns out to be quite an expensive affair. However, if you hold debt mutual fund units for a period of 3 years or above, they qualify to be long-term assets and the overall gains from them get taxed at 20% after allowing for inflation indexation. For example, if you invested 100 rupees in FY 2013-2014 and you earn an interest of 10% every year, the final amount at the end of 3 years after taking into effect all of the above factors (assuming the income tax bracket of 30% and ignoring other cess) are as follows:

Scenario 1 – Direct holding of the security with cumulative interest

Effective interest amount p.a. after 30% tax = 10% x (1 – 30%) = 7%

Total value at the end of 3 years net of tax = 100 x $(1 + 7\%)^3$ = 122.5

Scenario 2 – Holding of debt fund with management fees @0.5% p.a.

Effective interest rate p.a. after fees = 10% x (1 – 0.5%) = 9.45%

Value at the end of 3 years net of fees = 100 $(1 + 9.45\%)^3$ = 131.11

Inflation index factor between FY 13-14 & FY 16-17 = (1125÷ 939)

Indexed cost of acquisition = 100 x (1125÷ 939) = 119.8

Capital gains = 131.11 – 119.8 = 11.31

Capital gain tax @ 20% = 11.31 x 20% = 2.26

Total value at the end of 3 years net of taxes and fees = 128.85

In this example, scenario 2 outshines scenario 1 by 5% over a 3 year period. This can also be considered as a margin of safety for the debt fund as it would be subject to actual performance falling short of the fixed rate which is known in the scenario 1, interest rate risks, fund manager's liquidity constraints due to possible excessive redemption, etc.

Considering all the above advantages, you may choose to invest the debt part of your asset allocation into a carefully chosen set of 2-3 diversified debt mutual funds, generally known as income funds. The process of selecting the funds could be similar to that explained in the previous chapter for equity mutual funds, using the 'sharpe ratio.'

At a glance . . .

- ₹ *A bank fixed deposit is a loan that you give to the bank.*
- ₹ *Investment in debt brings in stability and predictability in cash flows and therefore plays an important role in the investment portfolio.*
- ₹ *Compounding works continuously and predictably only in fixed income instruments, since future returns do not have the power to erode past returns.*
- ₹ *There is nothing called risk-free instruments; only the context and scope of risk changes.*
- ₹ *Default risk represents the possibility of the entity taking the loan not being able to repay the same.*
- ₹ *Reinvestment risk refers to the rate of interest on a similar debt instrument being different from what was in the previous one, upon reinvestment of the maturity proceeds.*
- ₹ *Interest rate risk arises when someone needs liquidity during the tenure of the instrument and the general interest rate fluctuations impact its value in the secondary market.*
- ₹ *Unlike equity, to have a diversified debt portfolio, it is better to hold a few debt mutual funds than to hold multiple debt instruments.*

18

DON'T PAY OFF YOUR HOME LOAN & LET THE WELL DRY UP

"While I encourage people to save 100% down for a home, a mortgage is the one debt that I don't frown upon."

– Dave Ramsey

One of the major liabilities that people acquire early on in their life is a home loan; and that too, for about a couple of decades. With the current real estate prices, this weighs down heavily on the financial health of a young family and is an emotional trauma for them. There is always the risk of uncertainty in their jobs and therefore the home loan is considered to be evil and a burden though it is a necessary one. The elders in the family try to make their young ones more 'responsible' by making them take a home loan, effectively trapping them and preventing them from contemplating a change in career as per their interests or exploring the possibilities of becoming an entrepreneur that can be effectively done only when they are young as they still do not have the responsibilities of raising a family. Blame the kids for not standing up for their dreams.

Anyhow this huge liability puts a lot of pressure on youngsters and there is a mad rush to 'finish off' this loan. A couple of myths about home loans also positively contribute to this urgency. The first one is regarding the interest component in the equated monthly installment (EMI). A large section of people believe that banks are crooks and they take away the interest of the entire tenure in advance and therefore, if at all you have to save that interest, you have to pay off the loan early. Else it is better to continue the loan till the very end. Why is this a myth? Banks cannot charge more interest than what is due for the period that they consider as rest or compounding frequency at any given point along the tenure of the loan. In the case of any loan to be repaid as EMIs, the rest will be every month.

For example, if the loan amount is 50 lakhs, interest rate is 12% p.a., and the tenure is 20 years, the EMI works out to be 55,054 rupees. However, for the first month, the interest due is 1% of 50 lakhs which amounts to 50,000 rupees. Therefore, from the EMI amount, 50,000 will be accounted as interest and the remaining 5054 as principal. The loan outstanding in the initial period is high and therefore the interest amount rightfully due is also high. As time progresses, the outstanding loan reduces considerably due to part payment of principal every month and triggers a virtuous cycle of interest component reduction and corresponding principal component increment in order that the EMI amount remains the same.

Therefore, you can be rest assured that throughout the tenure of a loan, the interest at any given point is paid only on the outstanding loan amount and hence there is no need to try and finish the loan early. Instead, after accounting for the EMI outflow, the surplus savings amount available should be accumulated and invested according to the asset allocation required for the target return strategy. Otherwise, your financial assets would dry up paying off the loan, thus leading to the unfavourable situation of being asset-rich and cash-poor. And in case there is some financial goal falling due in between that requires liquidity, it wouldn't be available and would lead to yet another unfavourable situation of having to take a personal loan or credit card loan at a higher rate of interest.

The second myth is about increasing the EMI contribution during the tenure. There are many who believe that increasing the EMI would lead to the bank taking away additional interest. As mentioned earlier, banks cannot take away more interest than what is due. Considering the earlier example, if instead of the calculated EMI of 55,054 rupees, if one decides to increase this EMI to say 60,000 rupees, even then only 50,000 rupees would be accounted as interest in the first instalment and the remaining 10,000 rupees will go into principal repayment.

Therefore, for those of you who still want the EMIs to be finished off early, there is a simple method that you may use so that your accumulation of financial assets is also not disturbed. This is to increase the EMI every year to the extent of the increment in income that you get. If the increment in income is 10%, EMI also goes up by 10%; if it is 5%, the same goes for the EMI; and if your income doesn't increase, there would be no change in EMI as well. Would you like to take a guess regarding how much the tenure will reduce to, from 20 years in the above example, if one decides to increase the EMI by 10% every year?

The answer is 8 years and 11 months; i.e. the loan EMI increased by just 10% every year gets the loan amount completely repaid in less than 9 years. And this is assuming 12% interest rate. If the prevailing rate of 8.5% is applied, the EMI reduces to 43,391 rupees (adding about 11,000 rupees p.m. to the investment portfolio) and the tenure reduces to 9 years and 8 months approximately.

Additionally, once the asset allocation is decided, you may also decide to take out a portion of money from the debt allocation and use the same to pay off the loan. For example, say the total investments for the current year is coming to

15 lakh rupees after taking out all the cash outflows, and the asset allocation is done as 40% Equity, 40% debt and 20% precious metals. This means that 6 lakhs will be invested in debt. Considering liquidity requirement in the near future, you may take just 2 or 3 lakhs out of the debt allocation and use it to pay off the loan, further reducing its tenure. This way we will ensure that we don't lack liquidity at any given point for other goals AND pay off the loan faster WITHOUT impacting the allocation that is required for all the asset classes.

Another feature provided by many banks nowadays is an overdraft account linked to the home loan into which you may park your surplus funds to reduce the interest amount charged. Using the above logic, once the asset allocation is made, instead of investing your money into debt funds separately, you may park this portion (as per the example above, 6 lakh rupees) in this overdraft account. However, there are a couple of more variables that need to be considered before trying to take advantage of this feature. Generally the bank charges a higher rate of interest for people who want to avail this facility. Further, the collective tax advantage you get in debt mutual funds as explained in the previous chapter and the reduction in tax deduction benefit you may enjoy on the loan interest need to be considered before using the overdraft facility.

For example, if you can earn 9% on debt funds that will be subject to long-term capital gains tax with the inflation indexation benefit and enjoy a direct 30% deduction in tax towards a similar interest paid on home loan, keeping the excess funds in the overdraft account may not make sense. However, if you are keeping this surplus liquidity while awaiting an investment opportunity in other asset classes, then the overdraft account will make more sense.

Therefore, repayment of home loan is not an impulsive decision but a carefully considered decision, preferably taken after consulting with a financial planner and doing the required calculations as applicable.

At a glance . . .

- ₹ *A large home loan at the beginning of one's career stifles the possibilities of taking risks and pursuing one's dreams.*
- ₹ *Banks cannot charge more interest than what is due for a given period at any point along the tenure of the loan.*
- ₹ *Once a home loan is taken it is generally better to continue paying the instalments while investing the surplus into a portfolio with the appropriate asset allocation.*
- ₹ *Prematurely paying off the home loan will lead to a situation of being asset-rich and cash-poor.*
- ₹ *If you want to finish your home loan earlier than planned, increase the EMI every year to the extent of the increment in your income.*
- ₹ *Once the asset allocation is decided, you may use a part of the debt allocation to pay off the loan without hurting liquidity.*
- ₹ *An overdraft account linked to the home loan into which you may park your surplus funds is a good idea to save interest costs.*
- ₹ *Repayment of home loan is not an impulsive decision but a carefully considered decision, taken after consulting with a financial planner and doing the required calculations as applicable.*

19

SAVING TAXES OR TAXING YOURSELF?

"Go out there and get rich. Get so obnoxiously rich that when that tax bill comes, your first thought will be to choke on how big a check you have to write."

– ***Mark Cuban***

In my career spanning over a decade and a half, I have not seen a single individual who is happy about paying taxes. I agree that it is painful, but if you look at the larger picture, it will turn out that taxes are not that bad after all. It is the income of the government, which is the most important driving factor of the economy. It provides buying power for a large section of our society, the government employees; including the defence forces, police, railways, the various government departments and autonomous regulatory bodies such as RBI, SEBI, etc. Also the government is the biggest spender in the economy through discharging its responsibility as the creator of the public infrastructure. Therefore, I am a big advocate of paying the appropriate taxes, though also a big critic of the complicated tax laws.

However, any possibility of saving taxes is easily lapped up by us without even considering the pros and cons of it. Yes, there are cons of tax benefits. Not all tax benefits actually turn out to be beneficial. For example, your investment in a public provident fund account is nothing but a long-term low interest loan given to the government. Other products such as insurance policies, unless bought in their purest forms, tend to nullify the benefits of tax saving due to their inherent inefficiencies as discussed earlier. Those who invest the maximum amount into such instruments deprive themselves of the possibility of investing in other asset classes and generate better returns over the long-term. I am not against investment in these instruments, but I definitely do not endorse the last minute unplanned decisions people take towards the end of the financial year just to save taxes. I also know of people whose contribution into their employee provident fund exceeds the tax deduction limit, but still end up putting the maximum possible amount into PPF in pursuit of guaranteed tax-free interest, thereby depriving themselves of the much needed liquidity during their high expense phase of life.

These are promoted as 'forced savings' by the older generation, and is considered as a virtue. But at what cost of opportunity and quality of life is something that needs to be thought about. Blind beliefs and general rules cannot become virtues unless applied according to the financial goals and circumstances of the individual. Just because a tax deduction limit opens up doesn't mean we should use it. It may make better sense to pay the taxes and invest the money appropriately in a portfolio that is properly diversified. For instance, a fresh tax deduction limit of 50,000 got opened up recently towards contribution to NPS. I recommend this to be utilized only by those individuals in the 30% tax bracket as it may otherwise mean too much money going into long-term locked-in investments.

Another way in which the government extends tax benefits is by promoting expenses. The housing sector gets a boost when people are given a tax break on the interest paid on home loans. But would it be wise for an individual to buy a second property on loan just because the first loan is over and the 'interest benefit' will be lost? What is the logic in creating a liability and incur interest expense on it just to save a portion of it in the form of taxes? Even if it is done with the intention of creating a long-term asset, shouldn't it be tested for its feasibility and impact on other financial goals before implementing it?

Businessmen relish the possibility of buying cars and other so-called 'assets' to get the benefit of depreciation. Even tax professionals promote such methods for saving taxes without putting much thought into the fact that such savings are brought about upon creating expenses which could be avoided. Isn't it better to pay 30% tax and retain 70% money which can be deployed in a better way? In short, what is the point in saving 30 rupees by spending 100 rupees? The resistance in paying taxes is what brings about such unnecessary expenses and drains away the financial energy of enterprises.

Now let's take up the point of our unwillingness to pay taxes leading us to have unaccounted income. This would not be called tax saving but tax evasion. For a moment let's forget the legal and ethical aspect of tax evasion and focus on its financial prudence. For instance, if you have unaccounted cash kept at home, it remains idle. Assuming you saved 30% in tax, it takes just 4 or 5 years in a fixed deposit to cover up the tax amount. After this, every rupee you earn is a profit. If you argue that the interest in fixed deposit is also taxable, my counter to that would be that the tax is paid from the interest income which was not getting earned when the cash was sitting idle at home. However, as discussed in the previous chapters, there are many other investment avenues such as debt mutual funds and stocks which can get you to break-even much earlier with very less tax on income generated further.

If not kept in cash, you would be deploying the unaccounted income in other assets like real estate or gold. However, the papers would carry a much lower value than what you paid, as the cash component cannot reflect there. The taxman would get hold of you the moment you want to liquidate these assets in the form of capital gains tax.

Also, you have lost the opportunity of deploying the money in high growth assets such as equity that would generate tax-free dividend incomes that are truly passive in nature. Those who put the tax evaded money into land are deprived of this passive income which, over a period of time, more than compensates for the tax paid.

I have a larger point to make here. Unless you have illegal sources of income such as drug peddling, extortion, corruption, etc., there is no long-term value in evading taxes. The biggest victims of the tax evasion thought process are professionals like doctors and lawyers who receive a lot of income in the form of cash and hence get lured into not disclosing such income.

As mentioned in the first chapter, if your income is unaccounted, your expenses will also go unchecked and that would create a huge financial leakage. And since the income is unaccounted, maintaining the paper trail for cross-checking becomes an extremely cumbersome process and such a trail will always remain a potential threat for getting caught. Sooner or later you will get tired of managing these transactions and this would lead you to splurge pompously on various occasions such as your children's marriage, etc. Within limits these expenses are of value, however, spending excessively to get rid of the money would definitely be bad planning. It would have been much better to spend 30% of it on taxes and preserve the remaining. And those who go to the extreme extent of buying properties in fictitious people's names eventually are bound to lose 100% of the value of their assets as succession planning is impossible on such properties.

Disclosing all the income and paying the correct taxes would open up a host of cleaner and better prospects that would not only preserve your assets but also grow them better. Further, it would also give you peace of mind as you are not committing any illegality. Not to mention the happiness and fulfilment you will naturally get owing to the positive contribution you made towards nation-building. Paying taxes honestly and correctly also helps in reducing inflationary impacts on the economy brought about by deficit financing, or in simple terms, the artificial printing of money by the government to bridge its shortfall. If the government has to resort to this method on a continuous basis in order to execute its developmental and people-friendly measures due to insufficient income generated through taxes, it will only come back to haunt us in the form of inflation that will lead to further deterioration of our wealth.

Therefore, it would be safe to conclude that trying to evade taxes is another example of being penny wise and pound foolish. Tax saving, on the other hand, should in fact be the by-product of a sound purpose-driven financial planning exercise instead of being an objective itself.

At a glance . . .

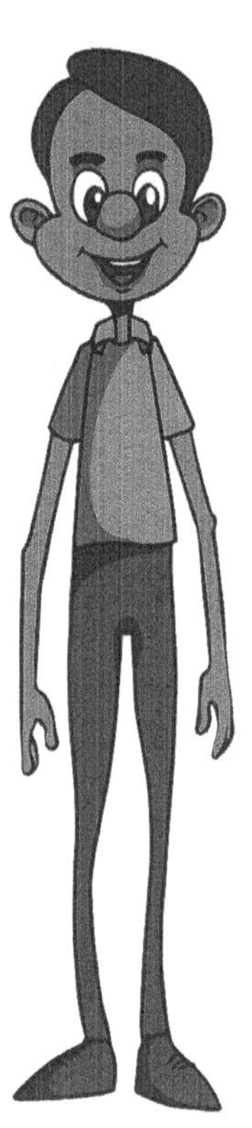

- ₹ *Paying taxes brings the money back into the economy through government expenditure and hence is a good idea.*
- ₹ *Not all tax benefits actually turn out to be beneficial.*
- ₹ *Taking last-minute unplanned decisions towards the end of the financial year just to save tax is an unhealthy practice.*
- ₹ *'Forced saving' has an opportunity cost associated with it.*
- ₹ *There is no point in incurring a fresh, unnecessary expenditure, only to be able to get some tax break on it.*
- ₹ *Tax evasion proves to be a very expensive affair in the long run in terms of loss of opportunity.*
- ₹ *Spending excessively to get rid of the unaccounted money is definitely bad planning.*
- ₹ *Disclosing all the income and paying the correct taxes would open up a host of cleaner and better prospects that would preserve your assets, grow them better and give you peace of mind.*
- ₹ *Tax saving should in fact be the by-product of a sound purpose-driven financial planning exercise instead of being an objective itself.*

20

WHY YOU SHOULDN'T DO IT ALL BY YOURSELF

"Do what you do best and outsource the rest."

– Marcus Buckingham

Subbu went for a haircut. It was a Sunday morning and there was heavy rush at the barber's. He sat there and started observing the barber. After a few people's haircut was done, Subbu thought to himself, 'Hey it seems to be easy. Even I can do this. Why should I pay him fifty rupees?' He sat there for some more time observing the barber and then slid out of that place. Once he reached home, he pulled a chair in front of the mirror, took a pair of scissors and a comb, sat down and started cutting his own hair. He felt really happy saving so much of money and by the time he was done, he was indeed a sight to see.

Was he successful in getting himself a haircut? The answer is yes. But was it good enough? It's nobody's guess. There are two points to be understood here. Firstly, he observed the barber for just an hour or two and thought he could do it himself. Secondly, even an expert hair stylist trained in the best of the best institute won't be able to give a haircut to herself due to obvious physical limitations.

'How does this situation correspond to handling one's own finances?' you may be thinking. In the twenty odd years of education that we receive, there is hardly any formal training on managing our money. It's just hearsay, glancing of newspapers and news channels, water-cooler discussions in the office, etc., that make up our financial wisdom. Add to that the confusing articles that keep cropping up on the internet and the extremely jargonized language in which the ideas are expressed, we literally have an overdose of information and very little applied knowledge. The fact that you picked up this book and have read this far only means one thing. You definitely are serious about your financial future and wouldn't hesitate to spend time and effort to educate yourself. However, doing your own financial planning has very similar limitations as that of giving yourself a haircut. If the limitation in haircut is physical, i.e. you can't see your own head as you can see others' heads, the limitation in managing your own investments is emotional in nature. We tend to lack the courage that is required to take tough decisions with our own money as we tend to get emotionally attached to it. In short, in both the situations you are blinded, therefore you lack the correct perspective.

For example, if you were to pursue your ambition of starting your own business by quitting your job, you may be having either of the two extreme emotions - fear or overconfidence. There are many who have been thinking of getting into a business of their own for ages but never mustered up the courage to do so. And there are many who jumped into a business after quitting a high paying job, only to find the harsh realities of running a business. However, taking a balanced decision would involve taking your realistic cash flows into account, figuring out the buffer that needs to be created, and identifying the appropriate time at which you may quit the job. And it would be incomplete without a back-up plan in terms of having a realistic cut-off time within which if the business doesn't take off as expected, you will get back to your job.

A simpler example would be about just cutting your losses in a wrongly picked stock or mutual fund. People tend to hold on to their bad investments waiting for them to recover, while selling off their good ones the moment they hit reasonable profit levels instead of exploiting their full potential. Throughout this book we have discussed various behavioural aspects that affect people's decisions about money. Many more such as herd mentality, confirmation bias, status-quo effect, proximity bias, etc., also play their part in emotionally challenging you in your financial decisions, the explanation of all of which is out of scope of this book.

You may be able to get somewhere on your own with respect to your financial journey, however, it would suffice to say that you need the help of an expert to make it more structured and qualitative, as well as to take those crucial decisions along the way.

I remember counselling a person years ago while I was conducting a financial health clinic for the employees of a multinational company. He was fed up with his job and was on the verge of quitting. And what did he have in mind as an alternative career? Share trading. He had attended some small time courses on this subject and truly believed he had developed a 'knack' of trading in stocks. He was even confident of making 2,000 rupees per day through this activity and was expecting to make 50k-60k per month. Also he was highlighting the fact that markets are open only for 5-6 hours compared to his average working day of 10 hours, in addition to spending 2 hours in traffic. However, when I alerted him that there were only about 20 trading days in a month considering weekends and other holidays, and therefore even if he succeeded in his daily target, he would reach only about 40k per month, he looked upset.

But when I added that in order to take the trading positions the next day, he would need to prepare for another 5-6 hours researching about opportunities, in addition to the 6 hours of live market, he was aghast as to why he didn't think of that before. I continued further telling him how he had to invest only his time in his job, whereas he had to invest his time as well as money to earn a reasonable income out of share trading. At the end of the session he was convinced that share trading was not an appropriate alternative career path for him.

We all need to understand that whatever we have chosen to be our primary career, for which we are formally trained as well, would give us the best return on our time investment. Therefore, all our efforts should be to enhance our primary career by constantly upgrading and up-skilling ourselves.

There is no fun in being a 'Jack of all trades, and master of none,' especially related to serious matters like personal finance or health. In the information age that we are living in, we have developed an addiction to seek out information on anything and everything. Music being one of my hobbies, when I hear a good song I have to know who sang it, who gave the music and so on, and I get those information within minutes on the internet. But it will be a disaster if you start treating your illnesses based on the information you get on the internet.

My doctor who is an Ayurvedic practitioner told me something so profound when I asked him about something that I read on the internet related to my problem for which I was seeking his medical advice. He said, 'There is a difference between information and applied knowledge. The data that you are talking about is based on various tests conducted that are statistical in nature. The results are derived on the basis of the probability of occurrence and let's say there is a 70 or 80% probability of something being the cause of an illness, then it is widely publicized and you will get that *information* easily on the internet. However the *knowledge* which your physician has would help him determine whether you belong to the 80% category or the 20% category.'

Similarly, you may apply to yourself the self-acquired information on financial planning and investments. However, only a professional financial planner would be able to sift through the information and provide you with a customized solution that will be efficient as well as effective with respect to your personal financial goals. Else, you may have to undergo formal training in financial planning and become an expert yourself, that would be quite a time-consuming affair. You just cannot become an expert with casual information.

There is yet another important reason why you shouldn't be doing it all by yourself. It is the difference between knowing and doing. Let me bring in an analogy here. We all know it is important to exercise, but how many of us are able to be disciplined with our workouts? An average gym would be selling multiple times the number of memberships than the number of people actually working out. The profitability of any gym depends heavily on the number of people not turning up for workouts as they can increase their revenues with the same capacity.

However, things get different when you hire a personal trainer. Firstly you get a target-oriented workout plan. And you can be sure about receiving a call when you don't turn up for a scheduled workout. There is continued motivation to go for the workouts; there will be a pre-workout routine and a post-workout routine that will prevent injuries and keep your muscles relaxed. Further, there will be constant enquiry regarding your diet because the trainer knows you might cheat. Add to that the challenges that he throws at you at will when he deliberately counts 9 three times before counting the 10th repetition in a set and the happiness you derive when you successfully complete those challenges, you know that you are very well on your way to accomplishing your goals. There are of course occasional disappointments when you are not able to complete a routine but you do have a shoulder to cry on that shares your pain and tells you 'it's okay.' But always remember, you have to do the hard work yourself and cannot blame the trainer for your failure.

Similar would be the result when you outsource your financial planning activity to a professional financial planner. There will be frequent audits and reviews, challenges thrown at you, with expert recommendations and customized solutions based on your financial goals. And most importantly, you get an intelligent sounding board for helping you take crucial financial decisions. But the onus is completely on you to implement the recommendations.

Also, with your otherwise busy schedules, it is practically impossible for most of you to be able to create a financial plan and stick to it. Being financially savvy is not at all difficult, but it requires your time, which is a rare and precious commodity. So it makes perfect sense for you to focus on your primary occupation and enjoy the weekends with your family, while your financial planner focuses on his primary occupation, i.e. creating your financial plan and helping you stick to it.

At a glance . . .

- *In the twenty odd years of education that we receive, there is hardly any formal training on managing our money.*
- *In this information age, we literally have an overdose of information and very little applied knowledge.*
- *Doing one's own financial planning is difficult as one may lack the emotional maturity and courage to take tough monetary decisions.*
- *Fear and overconfidence are the two emotions that interfere with one's soundness of judgement when it comes to monetary decisions.*
- *Our primary career, for which we are formally trained, would give us the best return on our time investment.*
- *Only a professional financial planner would be able to sift through the information and provide you with a customized solution that will be effective as well as efficient.*
- *You just cannot become an expert with casual information.*
- *A financial planner can help you to bridge the gap between knowing and doing.*
- *Focus on your primary occupation and enjoy your time with your family, while your financial planner focuses on his primary occupation, i.e. creating your financial plan and helping you stick to it.*

21

PAY YOU WILL FOR ADVICE – DIRECTLY OR INDIRECTLY

"Beware of false knowledge; it is more dangerous than ignorance."

– George Bernard Shaw

After a visit to a few government offices to get some documents readied, Subbu was very tired and too hungry to go back home to have lunch. So he walked into a restaurant. He was a changed man after his father's passing and had become too frugal with money, to the extent of being stingy. At the entrance itself there were two doors in which were written INDIAN and CONTINENTAL respectively. 'Indian would be cheaper,' he thought and walked into that door, only to find two more doors in front of him. They had VEGETARIAN and NON-VEGETARIAN written on them. 'Non-veg would be expensive,' he thought and walked into the vegetarian section. Again there were two doors, and interestingly, they carried the names PAID and FREE! Subbu was ecstatic and ran through the FREE door, and to his shock, only to find himself on the road.

The new business models in the world of internet use a lot of freebies to acquire new customers. Many of them are genuine, as is evident through the heavy losses reflecting on their balance sheets. However, not all deals that look free are actually free. It's only that the cost is recovered indirectly. Most of the five-star hotels offer a complimentary breakfast. If you look closely, this is just a ploy to ensure that the breakfast business wholly comes to them. Once the guest leaves the hotel for work, it is highly unlikely that he will return for lunch or dinner. However, breakfast is well within their control and if they keep it paid, guests may prefer to go for cheaper options outside. In short, when someone says breakfast is complimentary, what it means is that the room tariff includes its cost.

The financial advisory industry is also ridden with this sort of indirect cost structure. However, it is presented in the form of free advice. Common sense should suggest that no one will spend his or her time for free especially when they are helping you to deploy your money. Now to understand the impact of such an indirect arrangement, let's do a role play.

Imagine that you are the person offering financial advice to a prospective client. Will you do it for free? Let's park the answer for the time being. If you happen to be getting paid indirectly, i.e. through commissions from the various investment product manufacturers, what would you be keener on 'suggesting' as your advice? The product with the highest commission or the one with very less commission but which is the most suitable for the client? Irrespective of your answer to this question, let me admit that I have seen a lot of honest financial intermediaries who would suggest the latter. But a larger number are those who would suggest the former. Would you then qualify this as unbiased advice? This is the most important question for you to answer.

In the above situation, if you reverse the roles and become the client, I am sure you would prefer to have the latter option as the solution. Let me give you a third option. What if there is an advisor who would cut through the clutter and act in your interest by suggesting you the correct solution? Also, he would be investing time and effort to explain to you the details of the solution, making you understand the nuances of it and how it aligns with your financial goals. Further, he is under the direct control of the highest investment regulatory body of India, The Securities & Exchange Board of India (SEBI).

But the caveat is that he would charge you directly a nominal fee towards the consultancy offered. Now the questions become bigger and more direct. Would you qualify this as unbiased advice? If yes, would you be willing to pay that fee directly?

As explained in the previous chapter, it would definitely be a good idea to outsource your financial planning requirements to a professional unbiased planner who would put you at the centre and accordingly prepare a sound financial strategy for you. Needless to say that such a person should be highly knowledgeable about the various options available in the market so that he is capable of suggesting you the purest and best solutions that also turn out to be cheaper in the long run, instead of restricting himself to the limited associations that he may have.

You may still want it free and may resort to two options. First is to rely on the salesperson who, with his limited knowledge, may provide you with an incomplete solution. This would be like consulting the chemist for the medicine you need so that you can save on the doctor's fees. The second option is to take complete responsibility for your financial planning yourself, get yourself formally educated and apply such knowledge to create and maintain your financial plan. This would be like going through the entire MBBS degree to treat oneself. And that too, just for saving the doctor's fees. It's not impossible, however, it sounds to be quite a complicated solution for a simple problem.

There is a bigger threat looming large on both these options. The threat is of false knowledge and half-knowledge respectively, which can have very dangerous consequences and may result in huge losses in terms of money or opportunities. By half-knowledge, I am not referring to your inability to understand the financial concepts. Quite possibly you may understand them better than even professional financial planners. However, the key is to apply them in the right way at the right time, which may be difficult for you owing to your primary occupation.

I had the opportunity to address the employees of a large IT company. At the end of the seminar, a young man came up to me and asked, "Why should I pay a fee to a financial planner? Can't I do my own financial planning?" I responded in the affirmative but asked him how he would do it. He said, "I have the weekends off and therefore have enough time to research, create the plan and then execute it." I welcomed the idea and asked him how much he would save as a percentage of his annual salary and his answer was, about 2%. I will leave you with the same question that I asked him for which he had no answer.

"Would you work two days every week for the whole year to save 2% of your salary, when you work five days every week to earn 100% of it?"

At a glance . . .

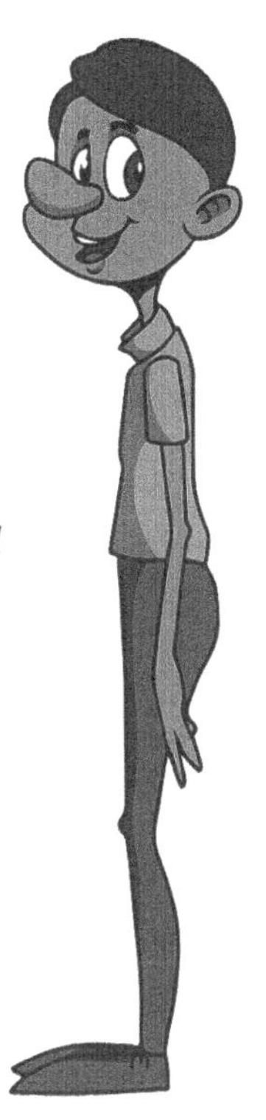

- ₹ *The financial advisory industry is ridden with an indirect cost structure, which is presented as free advice.*
- ₹ *Common sense should suggest that no one will spend their time for free especially when they are helping you to deploy your money.*
- ₹ *The paramount requirement while taking financial advice is for it to be unbiased; and it is rarely so if the advisor is commission-based.*
- ₹ *Develop the willingness to pay for financial advice directly for it to remain unbiased.*
- ₹ *False knowledge and half-knowledge entail high costs in terms of huge financial losses or loss of opportunities that may be reduced by paying the appropriate price to a knowledgeable professional.*

22

INVEST IN YOURSELF

"If a man empties his purse into his head, no man can take it away from him. An investment in knowledge always pays the best interest."

– Benjamin Franklin

Subbu was trying hard to cut a tree with an axe. He was trying really hard, sweating all over. A passerby suggested to him that he would be able to do it easily with a chainsaw. Subbu bought a chainsaw and continued his work. In the evening when the same person passed by him again, he was surprised that the tree was still not cut and a tired and frustrated Subbu was sitting with a very grim face. Upon seeing the passerby Subbu angrily walked up to him and said, 'You cheated me. This thing doesn't work." The passerby took a look at the chainsaw and pushed a button and it whirred into action. Subbu exclaimed, "What is that sound?"

So far we have focussed our energies on what to do after the money is made. But what about the most important asset, which is the source of your income; i.e. yourself.

We have infinite potential within us to be productive by acquiring new skills, which when applied can be monetized to give us a very high return on our time investment. Like Subbu, who because of his ignorance wasn't able to extract the maximum potential out of the chainsaw, you may not be extracting the full potential you may have. However, acquiring those skills requires you to invest money and time on a regular basis outside your normal work schedule. These skills need not necessarily be related to the work that you do, but may add tremendous value to your personality and may come in handy at the most unexpected of times. For example, if you learn a new language of your interest, neither with any specific goal in mind nor necessitated by the project that you are working on currently, it may come into use in a totally different project at a different time or may help you to interact with a prospective client that may land you a good deal.

There should be a regular allocation in your financial plan, for self-improvement and skill development ideally to the extent of 5% of your annual income. This allocation will pay for your seminars, training and certification programs, webinars, books, etc,. that would help you improve yourself and acquire new skills. These may appear to be expense heads, but in reality they are an investment in your career.

Human body is nothing but a machine with emotions and its own little quirks. And therefore it has to be taken good care of to be able to perform at its fullest. Investing in oneself would include providing the body and mind with a healthy lifestyle. The key factors to consider here are listed below:

A Timely & Balanced Diet – However busy you are, there is no excuse for not having your food on time. It is also important that we keep the food balanced with ample provision for pulses, whole fruits and vegetables, to give us a liberal dose of proteins, vitamins, minerals and fibre. And use organic produce as much as possible. They may be expensive, but are really worth it in the long run.

Nutritional Supplements – This is a legitimate shortcut to fill the unavoidable nutritional gaps due to various reasons that are beyond our control. Apart from being exposed to UV light, we are also vulnerable to various pollutants through air, water, and food that create a lot of free radicals in our body. These free radicals are the key reason for a number of degenerative diseases like heart ailments, cancer, diabetes, arthritis, etc., that make your body rust from within. Investing in nutritional supplements is the true way to get your health and your family's health insured as they supply you with a basket of antioxidants that help in neutralizing the free radicals and truly prevent the degenerative diseases from afflicting you. The return on this investment is the quality additional time that you get to live and enjoy life to the fullest. *Traditional medicine only extends the life of a diseased body. Nutritional medicine extends the life of a healthy body.*

To get a more authentic explanation on the importance of nutritional supplements, I would highly recommend you to read the book titled "What your doctor doesn't know about nutritional medicine may be killing you," by Dr. Ray D. Strand, MD.

Adequate Sleep – We all know the importance of shutting down our electronic gadgets periodically to enhance its efficiency. However, many of us tend to fool ourselves with the 'work hard, party harder' philosophy that takes a toll on our health. We all need 6-7 hours of sleep every night that rests and rejuvenates our body for a fresh beginning the next day. This will help us to avoid burning out early. Imagine the wealth you would create, if you add a quality additional five years to your career. That's a decent return for sleeping well, right?

Moderate Exercise & Periodic Body Massage – Have you heard the saying 'use it or lose it'? Moving all our joints and muscles in the aerobic and anaerobic zone helps us to enhance their optimal functioning life by a number of years. And the investment required for this is a mere 3-4 hours a week. And what we need to have is a planned whole-body workout. This may include getting a health club membership and even a personal coach for this purpose. So there is investment in terms of money as well. But the returns far exceed this investment in the long run.

To know how to plan your workout, please read the book "Don't Lose Out Workout!" by Rujuta Divekar.

Getting a full-body massage done once a month or two helps all the muscles to relax and work in pristine condition. This may help you relax your mind as well.

Periodic Health Check-ups – Early detection of diseases plays a critical role in treating them successfully. Therefore, it is highly recommended that a complete medical check-up is done once every year at a reputed diagnostic centre. They usually have different packages designed for people at different life stages based on the critical health risks they may face. Choose the most exhaustive one that suits your life stage and you can even avail a tax benefit for this.

Mental health is all about helping our mind to remain productive and requires us to consciously invest our thought energy and time in the following ways:

A Positive Attitude – It helps us to objectively look for solutions in adverse circumstances and eliminates the unnecessary stress created due to worrying. It also makes us enjoy the present, be hopeful about the future and brings in energy and enthusiasm.

An Attitude of Gratitude – Counting our blessings and being grateful for them everyday makes us focus more on what we have rather than what we don't have and brings peace to our mind. Doing this as a conscious activity before sleeping also helps our body get the required amount of quality sleep.

Meditation – For those who can keep still for even a minute, this may work. Slowly you can work at increasing the time period of this stillness as the main thing is to keep the mind relaxed and as a mere witness, to just observe the numerous thoughts that fly in and out. This is more entertaining than the Game of Thrones as you will be amazed at the quantum of useless thoughts that keep nagging you unconsciously and drain you of your vital energy.

Quality in Work – Mental health is normally connected to relaxation and de-stressing, which is quite true. However, I have observed that even accomplishing your daily tasks in an effective manner not only makes you happy, but also energizes your mind. So, whatever you do, however mundane and repetitive it may be, put absolute quality into it and see how your mind enjoys it thoroughly. Brian Tracy has written a gem in the form of 'Eat That Frog.' Grab it today to get into a world of enhanced productivity and avoid the cancer called procrastination.

Hobbies, Interests & Non-interests – As much as putting quality into even mundane work energizes your mind, giving it variety through pursuing your hobbies and passions keeps it fresh and happy. Even things you are NOT interested in, provide your mind with the requisite variety. So, you may periodically take up for a short while, stuff which you would otherwise be not interested in pursuing. This will also enhance your general knowledge and make you versatile. This versatility will positively contribute towards enhancing your social health in terms of being able to help others with your knowledge or in the least to build a good conversation with people.

Take a pause here and reflect on these points for a while. May be write down the list of excuses that you may have for not maintaining a healthy lifestyle, and take another step forward to find one reason why you should. I'm sure you can find one.

We all have heard the adage health is wealth. Of course it is, but financial wealth matters too. However, it would pay to always remember this:

Never make your wealth by losing your health. If you do so, spending your entire wealth also may not help you restore your health.

At a glance . . .

- ₹ *You are your most important asset.*
- ₹ *Invest in your career through regular allocation in your financial plan for self-improvement and skill development.*
- ₹ *Human body is nothing but a machine with emotions and therefore requires to be taken good care of to be able to perform at its fullest.*
- ₹ *Invest in nutritional supplements to ensure your body gets all the nutrients that it needs to keep itself fully functional. This is true preventive medicine and health insurance.*
- ₹ *Invest 3-4 hours every week on exercise and 6-7 hours every day on sleep.*
- ₹ *Mental health is all about helping our mind to remain productive and requires us to consciously invest our thought energy and time.*
- ₹ *Apart from hobbies and interests, you may from time to time take up for a short while, stuff which you would otherwise be not interested in pursuing. This will make you versatile and contribute towards enhancing your social health.*

23

THE EYE OF DEATH

"In this world nothing can be said to be certain, except death and taxes."
– Benjamin Franklin

How much ever we try to protect and grow our wealth, death is going to take it all away from us one day. The eye of death is constantly on your wallet and has the capacity to rob you of all that you have at any time. Hence it is important that we take succession planning very seriously and ensure that the inter-generational wealth transfer happens smoothly. I have seen many in my career who keep postponing succession planning as they do for insurance. All I can say is that they haven't yet come to terms with this ultimate reality. The most important question that people have in their mind is about when they should start their succession plan.

In reality, succession planning starts the moment one acquires any asset in the form of including a nominee or joint holder as part of the entailing documentation. Even doing this much in a careful manner ensures that the transfer of wealth happens without much difficulty. The catch however, is that strictly legally speaking, the nominee is only the custodian of the asset and does not become the de-facto owner of it. Any legal heir can claim their share of the asset from the nominee through initiating appropriate legal procedure. Therefore, I suggest people to start with independent succession planning as soon as they have accumulated some reasonable assets which they would like to segregate and distribute to different individuals.

A 'will' written by the owner of the assets on a legally valid sheet of paper that is witnessed by a couple of people and is registered with the concerned authority is the simplest method of letting the world know how you want to distribute your wealth. For many, however, the worry remains whether the successors would be capable of preserving and managing those assets, especially in the event of the successors being minors or differently abled. In such a scenario, forming a trust would be a good solution. In a trust, there is no complete transfer of ownership of the asset that takes place immediately. Only the benefits arising from the assets such as rental or dividend income get transferred to the beneficiaries. A trust is managed by a group of trustees that you have the freedom to appoint. The trustees will never have the rights of the assets, but only the authority to manage them. Even a life insurance policy can be assigned to a trust, if the insured person doesn't want the entire insurance proceeds to land up in the hands of the heirs in one stroke, in order to avoid any possibility of misuse or mismanagement. The various purposes for which such funds shall be used along with the timelines for the same may also be specified under a trust.

It is important for many people especially businessmen to ensure that their life insurance proceeds are not attached against any financial liability that they may be holding. For this purpose, at the time of taking the insurance policy, it may be put under MWPA (Married Women's Property Act). This ensures that the insurance proceeds go only to the wife of the deceased and such funds cannot be attached to settle any of the liabilities of the deceased. This is also an important aspect of succession planning.

A will once written can be changed any number of times and therefore, there is no point in waiting till a particular age to write it. Once written keeping in mind certain assets, it can be updated on a regular basis as and when one keeps acquiring newer assets or changing the form of existing assets. In the absence of proper succession planning by the asset holder, the applicable succession act will come into force and the wealth will be distributed according to the provisions of law. However, in the current system, that is quite a time-consuming affair and cumbersome for the family to manage.

It is therefore highly recommended that appropriate succession planning measures are undertaken while a person is alive, and that too, by taking proper consultation from a trustworthy legal expert so that nothing is left to chance. There are stories of the other extreme too. There are those who write a will and keep it in such a place that is unknown to anyone because they don't trust anyone. There is no use of such a succession planning exercise. It is important to have a close confidante with whom you can share the details of your succession documents. This should ideally be your spouse or one of the trusted family members or the legal professional who prepared the document. Once you do this, you will be relieved of one of your most important responsibilities, that of protecting your wallet even after you are gone; i.e. you would have actually cheated death, albeit in a different way.

At a glance . . .

- ₹ *The eye of death is constantly on your wallet and has the capacity to rob you of all that you have at any time.*
- ₹ *Succession planning starts the moment one acquires any asset in the form of including a nominee or joint holder as part of the entailing documentation.*
- ₹ *Strictly legally speaking, the nominee is only the custodian of the asset and does not become the de-facto owner of the same, hence necessitating a formal succession planning arrangement.*
- ₹ *Wills and trusts are the most commonly used succession planning tools that may be used according to one's specific needs.*
- ₹ *MWPA (Married Women's Property Act) is a very important tool that can be used to protect life insurance proceeds from being attached against other financial liabilities of the insured person.*
- ₹ *In order to avoid the legal hassles of succession, it is highly recommended that appropriate succession planning measures are undertaken while a person is alive, by taking proper consultation from a trustworthy legal expert so that nothing is left to chance.*
- ₹ *It is important to have a close confidante with whom you can share the details of your succession documents so that they can be found easily if and when the need arises.*

24

YOUR WALLET OF TIME

"As a well-spent day brings happy sleep,
so a life well-spent brings happy death."

– Leonardo da Vinci

We have a limited life span. That is, our wallet of time is a fixed quantity which is unknown to us. Therefore, it is most important for us to live a life of purpose and use our money and wealth in a constructive way so that it continues to serve humanity. We wear a lot of masks in our life; that of our education, profession, being a high-flying executive, social status, big cars, houses, expensive clothes and the list goes on. And it is but natural for us to closely identify with them. However, with time, a realization that we are beyond these masks should also set in that will make us live consciously every moment of our life. Only then we will be able to look at time, money and wealth in a dispassionate manner and will develop the maturity to use them with the larger interest of the world that we live in.

Many of us spend our lifetime accumulating and preserving wealth for our future generations. But what good is such wealth which is received on a platter and that takes away the drive from the next generation to succeed and script one's own life story? I am not saying that you shouldn't keep anything for your future generations. The previous chapter was fully about that, wasn't it? And remember Subbu's father? He knew there had to be a contingency plan, but he kept the crucial information away from his son and delivered it to him only after he had learnt a hard life lesson. Similarly, along with creating wealth for them, we should focus on providing our children with the right knowledge about money and wealth so that they grow up into responsible and empathetic human beings. They should grow up understanding the hard fact of life that not everyone in this world gets the same opportunities and are as privileged as they are.

Unfortunately we live in a world where, on one hand there are people who selfishly accumulate wealth even by putting others to heavy disadvantage, and on the other hand are those who in their urge to attain spiritual growth look down upon money and wealth. This is also a very dangerous attitude because it kills enterprise and the value of being productive. The wrong understanding of the 'ultimate truth' runs deep in our part of the world.

Subbu was lying idle on the couch watching his favourite television program when his friend's father who was a very successful man came to visit his family. Subbu's mother asked him to give his valuable advice to her son so that he did something worthwhile with his life than to idle away his time. Subbu was called in, and the man asked him, 'Why don't you do any work?' Subbu replied, 'What will happen if I work?' The man replied patiently, 'If you work hard, you will make money and become successful.' Subbu asked , 'What will happen if I am successful?' The man explained to him how he would be socially recognized, have a family, raise the family, get his children settled and eventually retire. Subbu persisted with his question, 'What will happen after that?' to which the man responded, 'After you retire, you can be stress-free and enjoy your favourite TV program lying on a couch.'

Subbu said, 'What do you think I was doing when you came in?'

This attitude is obviously flawed as it was possible for him to be in the couch all day because his parents were providing for him. But going beyond the realm of mere survival, we should all be looking at the attainment of personal fulfilment and happiness, which is impossible without the following two aspects:

Firstly, exploring and finding out our true passion in life and pursuing it with all our might without getting distracted by the various masks that come along the way, and at all times keeping our humility alive and our ego in check.

And secondly, by taking on the higher responsibility of helping and enabling others to live at least a dignified, if not a successful life. You have to respect your wallet of time and instead of squandering it away, it needs to be utilized well, not only to build your own wealth but also to be able to give back to the society. Many great souls who have walked this planet have emphasized on self-actualization as the ultimate goal of life and that can happen only if we are able to outgrow our selfish needs and are able to look beyond ourselves. We can easily find that the truly wealthy people in this world are engaged most of their time in philanthropic activities or have set aside a major portion of their wealth towards this purpose. They understand the secret that succeeding alone is no success at all. Until the entire humanity succeeds as a whole, an individual cannot be called successful.

Your wallet of time will become empty irrespective of whether you do something constructive with it or not. And there is no way in which you can reclaim the lost time. However, it will definitely make a lot of sense if whatever is left of it can be used to find your passion and pursue it to live a fulfilled life with each cell of your body brimming with happiness when you leave this world for the heavenly journey, knowing fully that you have indeed contributed towards making this world a better place to live.

At a glance . . .

- ₹ *Our wallet of time is a fixed quantity which is unknown to us.*
- ₹ *Just like spending money, spending time is also a pleasurable experience only if we do so mindfully.*
- ₹ *The 'me time' works wonders in terms of quietening down our mind which otherwise is constantly chirping away in its madness.*
- ₹ *If we spend too much time to earn money or waste it mindlessly, we will be left with too little time to live a life of purpose.*
- ₹ *Only when we live consciously every moment of our life, we will be able to look at time, money and wealth in a dispassionate manner and will develop the maturity to use them for the larger interest of the world that we live in.*
- ₹ *To those who spend their lifetimes accumulating and preserving wealth for their future generations, the question to be asked is, "What good is such wealth that is received on a platter and which takes away the drive from the next generation to succeed and script one's own life story?"*
- ₹ *Spirituality has nothing to do with financial prudence.*

- ₹ *Going beyond the realm of mere survival, we should all be looking at the attainment of personal fulfilment and happiness.*
- ₹ *You have to respect your wallet of time and instead of squandering it away, it needs to be utilized well, not only to build your own wealth but also to be able to give back to the society.*
- ₹ *Succeeding alone is no success at all.*